USER DRIVEN CHANGE:

GIVE THEM WHAT THEY WANT

Carlos del Rio & Jeff Noethen

User Driven Change: Give Them What They Want
© UD Publishing

Copy Editor: Emily Colangelo
Illustration: Carlos del Rio

Notice of Rights

All rights reserved. No part of this book may be reproduced or transmitted in any form by any means electronic, mechanical, photocopying, recording or otherwise without the written permission of the publisher. For information on obtaining permission for reprints of excerpts please make contact through www.udpublishing.com.

Notice of Liability

The information in this book is distributed on an "As Is" basis, without warranty. While every precaution has been taken in preparation of this book, neither the authors nor publisher shall have any liability to any person or entity with respect to any loss or damage caused or alleged to be caused directly or indirectly by the instructions contained in this book or by software, hardware or other products describe in it.

Trademarks

Throughout this book trademarks are used, and best attempts are made to indicate the proper trademark. All trademarks are used in an editorial fashion only and to the benefit of the trademark owner with no intention of infringement of the trademark. No such use, or use of any trade name is intended to convey endorsement or affiliation with this book.

ISBN: 978-0-578-01067-0

Dedications

Carlos: *This is for my sister who loves me in spite of my dedicating a book to her that she has no reason to read.*

Jeff: *To those people who have always told me that I can do anything that I put my mind to.*

CONTENT

Dedications _____ *3*

User Driven Change _____ *6*

  What *is* user driven change? _____ **7**

  How Do You Get Where You Are Going? _____ **9**
    Things To Keep in Mind _____ 17

  Your Home Page, An Important Landing Page _____ **17**

  Stand Alone Landing Pages _____ **18**

  Mini-Site, Robust Landing Pages _____ **18**

  Entrance to Site _____ **19**

  Customer Types _____ **20**

  Getting Visitors to Your Site _____ **24**

  Organic Search _____ **26**
    The Top 20 Travel Phrases By Monthly Volume (as of June 2008) ____ 26

  The Importance of Paid Search _____ **30**

  Offline Advertising _____ **32**
    Monthly Brand Searches According to Google™ _____ 32
    What to Look For in the Following Chapters _____ 33

All Above the Fold _____ *34*
    Total Page Layout _____ 37
    Content Change _____ 38

  Analysis _____ **40**

  Now What? _____ **50**

All About Speed _____ *52*

  Analysis _____ **59**

  Now What? _____ **66**
    A Minimal Site Requires Maximal Competency _____ 66

All About the Customer _____ *71*

  Site Design _____ **73**
    Positives: _____ 73
    Negatives: _____ 75

  Off-site Issues _____ 77

Things That Will Tip the Scales _____ 79
  Communication _____ 81
  Usability Testing _____ 81

Analysis _____ 83

Now What? _____ 90

All About Retention _____ 92

Site Design _____ 94

Communication _____ 99

Analysis _____ 101

Now What? _____ 108

Bringing These Ideas Together _____ 110
  How Do People Who Are Hungry for Accomplishment Behave? _____ 111
  How Do People Who Want to Be Taken Care of Behave? _____ 112
  How Do People Who Want a Connection to Other People Behave? _____ 112
  How Do People Who Want to Feel a Sense of Trust Behave? _____ 113
  How Do People Who Want Information Behave? _____ 113
  Guidelines for Web Communications _____ 114

A Note for Small Businesses _____ 117

Build Some Traffic _____ 119

Make Your Analysis in Context _____ 124

Do Some User Testing _____ 125
  Think About Methods, Not Band-Aids _____ 127

Glossary of Terms _____ 129

Index _____ 131

User Driven Change

"The business schools reward difficult complex behavior more than simple behavior, but simple behavior is more effective."

-Warren Buffet

"I don't look to jump over 7-foot bars; I look around for 1-foot bars that I can step over."

-Warren Buffet

Warren Buffet is definitely a man who has a head for business. He can lay out simple wisdom that is still hard to follow. However, we should look to live his advice; take the trails, and not the sheer rock wall; live in the simple, honest answers.

You've found this book because you are either thinking about making a change to your website, or like us, you are interested in increasing your knowledge base. Starting a project is simple because there are thousands of pages written, on the web and in print, that cater to beginners. There is a wealth of information that speaks to the advanced practitioner. But what about those who fall in between these two groups? We feel there is a gap in the information that is available, so we have created material that we feel suits an audience that has been working in the Internet arena for two to five years. This book does not tell you how to build a site, design a product, and build content. It lays out pragmatic plans for renovating four businesses in a competitive industry to demonstrate an issue that is on the horizon in business, and gives you actionable suggestions to help you understand and react to your customers.

Our goal is to describe these issues to people we would hire to work with us. We assume that you have enough knowledge about the Internet that we don't need to explain the concept, only the new approaches. Every concept is ramped quickly into intermediate knowledge and focuses there, explaining how we would test the data, implement changes, and track the effects. We end each section with some grander scale vision of the concept for those of you pushing your skills into expert level.

We base each approach off the assumption that your analytics data has shown a flaw in your website, or your end results are below expectations. Each approach varies depending on what your data is telling you. In addition to analytics data, you can also use your customer opinion data and any usability studies that you have done to determine what changes you should make.

What *is* User Driven Change?

Throughout this text, our stance is that the changes you make should be predicated upon data and input gathered from your customer. If you do not keep your customer in mind when changing your website, the results can be resoundingly negative. At the very least, you could lose any potential new customers and their resulting sales. At the very worst, you could see a highly negative viral campaign spring up via blogs and other forms of messaging that you have no way of controlling.

One of the best ways to know whether your customer will embrace your proposed site is to become a customer yourself. You do this in everyday life outside of work already. Remember when you were at the store and you wished the employee would stop goofing off with the other employee and come ask you if you needed help? Remember when you went online to pay your cable bill and couldn't figure out where the pay button was? These instances will happen to your customer if you do not take the time to ensure that your website makes sense to a first time user.

If you aren't savvy as to what a customer might or might not like about your website, hopefully you have an analytics tool that provides you with data and metrics that you can use to determine interaction, engagement, and conversion of your website. In some cases you can refer to your customer opinion data, if your site has this feature. Customer opinion data is a great way to get actual opinions straight from the customer's mouth, but this kind of reporting is sometimes skewed toward only vocal customers—not the majority. Also you may have to take a lot of it in stride because customers are more apt to leave negative feedback than they are positive feedback. However, many times you will be able to tell very easily if there is a certain feature or page that is not working well for your customers.

Usability testing is a great way to find out first hand from your customer if a particular design element is intuitive. If you don't have any of those tools or options, you can always scour the internet for blog postings from individuals to see if anyone is posting anything (good or bad) about your site. Keep in mind that "the customer is always right" does not mean that the customer should always get away with the loot. It means if you don't know your customer, your KPI's[1] will reflect this in the data and worse, your customers may talk to each other about it.

So, as we go through each chapter we use this approach of taking the customer's point of view to make changes to enhance the website. You'll see many of the tools listed above in our suggested measurements. Again, our hope is that this text is tailored to an intermediate practitioner, so most of the above should not need further definition. However, when in doubt please refer to the appendix for more information about any metric described in this text.

How Do You Get Where You Are Going?

Travel is complicated and, not surprisingly, the travel industry is fairly saturated. However, if you are a small business you cannot just stop here and give up. How can a business operating in a saturated industry differentiate their offering? How can you tell what's wrong? How can you tell if the changes you made worked? These are the questions that we will help you answer. You will see these concepts laid out in the answers to four other questions. If you already know which way you want to take your business, or are currently engaged in a project, feel free to skip directly to the chapter that best suits your immediate needs. However, we do suggest looking over the analytics sections for all four regardless of your circumstances—so you can be armed with information for planning future campaigns. Also, keep in mind that these methods are not industry-specific and aren't necessarily specific to a saturated industry. Your company might

---

[1] Key Performance Indicators

be the only company in the industry, but that does not mean that your website never has to be updated.

How can you make a site that is **quick to use and engaging?** *Time is money; if they spend less time they will spend time more often.* In the first review, we show how a fast website (including fast load time, fast page interaction time, ease of use to get through the process) helps lead to a better visitor experience. Some of the main talking points include:

- Site Speed—page load, functionality, usability of features
- Short Action Process—get me to your main point!
- Intuitive Design—does my site make sense for my intended customer?
- Clear Messaging—is it clear what I'm offering?
- Compartmentalization—are you quickly segmenting users by their immediate needs?
- Third-Party Integration—how can you capitalize on outside features from other companies to make my website a formidable player in the market?

As with all chapters we wrap up by explaining how you can test and measure the successes of the above.

How do you create a site that is **simple to use?** *Keep it simple and they will be done before they think about it.* In this review, we describe how taking away unnecessary portions of a landing page and keeping all options above the fold can provide a desirable visitor experience.

- Site Speed—how long does it take for the page to load or for a feature to render?
- Site Design—are you giving the customer too many options? What is your main point?
- Intuitive Functions—is the customer making it to the end goal? Am I driving conversion?
- Clear Brand—is this site recognizable and is it memorable to offline channels (television, print media, etc)
- Low Distraction—what are my main points of interest?

How do you create a site that is **very inviting?** *Everyone wants to be special; make them feel special.* In the third review, we describe how ensuring good customer service, including proper linking, categorization, and sound functionality can provide a desirable visitor experience.

- Customization—use of possessive links on-site: "My Account"
- Logged In Function—how does the site differ when a user is logged in versus logged out?
- Offline Presence—how else are customers remembering to come to my site?
- Special Offers—yes, customers are looking for the best deal, but how is my site different?

In today's "me" society, how can my site stand out for those customers willing to make a commitment to my site?

How do you create a site that is **hard to leave?** *If you treat them right they won't think of anyone else.* In the final review, we describe what features of a website will help to build a lasting relationship with your customer to retain them and keep them from visiting your competitor.

- Invitation—how do you get them in the door?
- Simplicity—customer acquisition often involves great features; keeping them usually involves making use of these features effortless.
- Compartmentalization—segment your users by need. Include alternate methods of interaction.
- Logged In Function—what makes being a member valuable?
- Third-Party Integration—again, making features/interaction effortless.

Ok, we have them hooked on the site, what next? Engagement metrics will tell you whether your supplemental tools are effective and whether your customers are interacting with these tools. These metrics include page views or elements viewed per session, event completion rate, and attribute metrics such as session length, subscribe rate, and customer rating.

How can you put this all together? What happens when you don't excel at any one metric? Functionally you will have limitations on what you can put in place. This is the special magic of analytics; they let you find out what is important to your users. There is a good deal of overlap in the type of changes that are made in each scenario; use this to your advantage. Review the behavior of your visitors to find out what they are looking for. Make the change that caters to the users' desires; again, that is what we call User Driven Change.

Analysis

If you are truly an intermediate analyst or above, you should have learned by now that with most analysis the metrics can be replicated for most projects. It's how you relay those metrics to your audience that defines the outcome. We use many of the same metrics for each case study, however, we show you how each metric is important to the main question in the case study and how each metric can show a different outcome when put in a different perspective.

We hope that by the end of this book you have a context to put your analytics in. Understanding where your users experience friction will give you very clear goals to accomplish and monitor. If you have further issues by the time you reach the end of this book I invite you to visit our website: UserDrivenChange.com. Ask follow up questions and leave your thoughts and next steps that you feel should be addressed.

All of our metrics align with the published draft of Web Analytics Definitions by the Web Analytics Association.[1]

---

[1] In September 2008, the Web Analytics Association posted a draft of Web Analytics definitions agreed upon by a WAA committee. This draft is open for public comment until December 31, 2008 and as such is not the final version at the time of our publication.

Landing Page Tactics

There are many articles and books written on best practices for landing page optimization. That is not necessarily what this book is about. However, for this book, here is our list of top ten tactics that a landing page should employ:

1. Clear path(s) for the visitor to follow to reach a desired goal.
2. Simple, effective navigation. Don't crowd the important areas with secondary levels.
3. Utilize supplemental tools such as onsite search and a Help link.
4. Color schemes and fonts—light background with dark text is the preferred method; utilizing your logo colors is advisable provided the color scheme makes the page easily readable.
5. Easy to find Customer service, account, site map links along with telephone contact information.
6. Personalization and empowerment terms such as "My Account," "My Shopping Bag," "My Itinerary," "My Bookings," etc.
7. Use of cookies and caching—the ability to know the customer and add personalization will not only aid the customer in their initial visit, but may also encourage them to sign up and/or return to the site for their future trip planning.
8. Appropriate use of Web 2.0 tools such as Flash and Ajax—these tools are great for branding and for long sell techniques, but we feel that they are best suited somewhere else in the site and not on the landing page; however, advertising tools such as mobile web, RSS etc. are highly recommended.

9. Make sure that your landing page is relevant to how the customer found you—don't have a paid search link for hotels land on the default page where airlines are selected.
10. Connect to people—post your awards (such as Customer Service Industry Leader, or Best Use of Web 2.0 Technology), or even include a spot for great customer feedback.

We then categorized this "best of breed" into four categories: all above the fold, all about speed, all about the customer, and all about retention.

Your business should have a unique value, and that means you have a unique customer base. Use all of the tools here to find the place where the concepts above work best for you. Keep in mind that some changes are mutually combative. Simple is not the same thing as fast; inviting is not the same as engaging. You will have to make concessions in some areas to keep your value remarkable in at least some aspect.

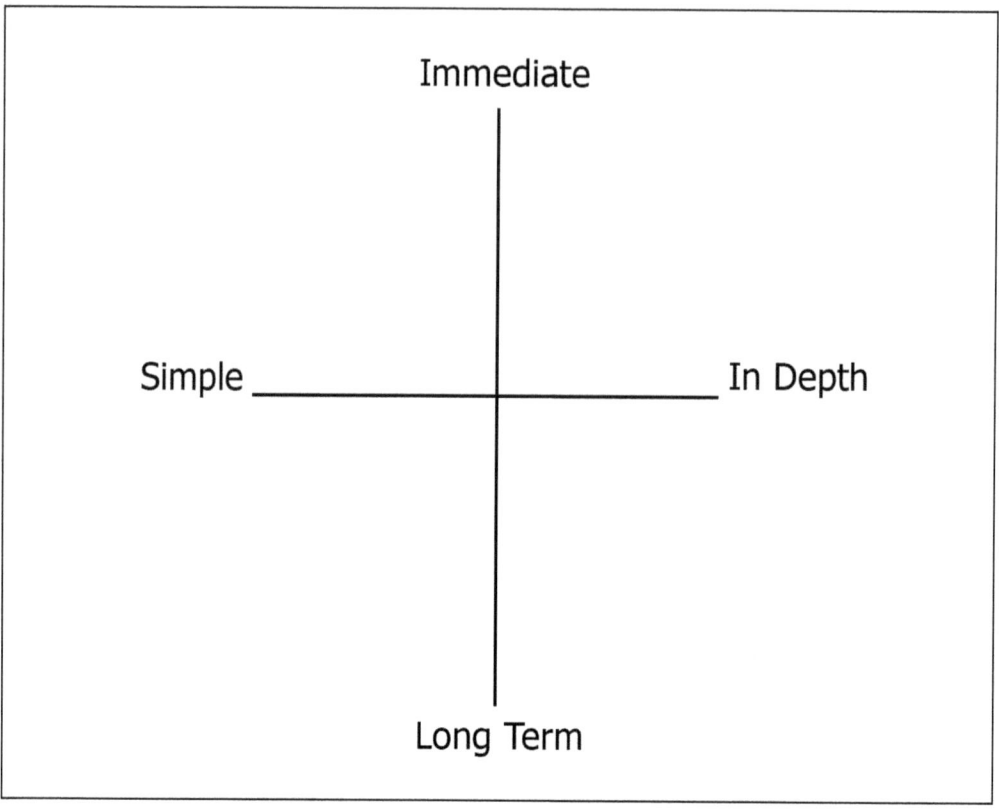

Because different people have different needs, you should choose where to aim based either on existing data or your sense of the business, and then take stock of response. In answering whether you have made the right decision you will discover where you should be headed. Customer acquisition and customer retention share some very obvious common elements. Fast and simple share some obvious common elements. Don't get overly worried about where to start. Choose something that can support more than one customer division and head toward the data that is strongest.

The end result should be a methodology for creating products/services that your customers can evangelize and consider link-worthy. User Driven Change will inspire and feed User Driven Marketing. The clearer your value and brand show in your site, the more linkable and sharable your content and service will be.

Things To Keep in Mind

Because we want this to be useful for websites in general we have four categories that we use to define the elements in your website:

Function Unit—this is an element that is used to drive primary objectives: sale, lead, information gathering, click, or download. The function is the promise that your site makes.

Up Sell Unit—taking your visitor from the initial promise to a bigger buy: sales, packages, accessories, and protection plans. Up sell are elements that increase to the level of business engagement.

Long Sale—elements that prolong the user engagement: RSS, newsletters, buyer clubs, credit card offers, contests, and logins. Long sale elements seek to embed your brand with the customer and inspire loyalty.

Protection—elements that assure the user: warranties, guarantees, certifications, etc. Protections are what keep the user safe.

Your Home Page, An Important Landing Page

Let's lay some groundwork for the following studies. There are three types of landing pages that you may be building: stand-alone, mini-sites, or entrance pages. This book looks at building entrance pages for full scale sites, and tracking their effects.

Stand-Alone Landing Pages

Most people have experienced this type of landing page in association with pay-per-click banner advertisements. This is the type that is frequently employed by e-books and lead generation sites. All of the information is given in one location usually with only one prominent call to action. Often the navigation is non-existent; the only way out is through taking action or via the back button. Generally these are created specifically for a given campaign. Stand-alone pages are very attractive to action-oriented people.

Mini-Site, Robust Landing Pages

Many large companies use mini-sites to showcase a specific type of item or to highlight a special offering. Mini-sites are frequently five to ten pages offering supporting material, echoing the call to action from the primary landing page. Often these pages will leverage the look and feel of the main site. Made for AdSense and Affiliate sites generally do not employ specific branding.

One of the positive features of mini-sites is their ability to give more information and make secondary calls to action without distracting the user. Mini-sites are better suited for researching/browsing users.

For example, SEObook.com and SEOmoz.org both provide a paid training program. Compare the two presentations. SEObook has a sales letter split into a tour with images, graphs, and rich media (video). SEOmoz has a shorter high-graphic presentation and testimonials that invite you to begin right away. Consider the different people who would respond to these pages. Who is going to click through several pages of text, watch videos, and look through graphs? Who is going to look at a New York Times review and sign up for a program? SEOmoz has a stand-alone page; SEObook has a mini-site within the main site.

Entrance to Site

Any page that a visitor arrives on is a landing page, even the pages in your main site. What does that mean to you? It means that you should have a clear purpose for your pages. Simply ask where you want to direct the visitor and make that the easiest exit from the page.

In some cases this can be difficult to accomplish. You likely have more than one thing that you want to offer. That is okay—just make one option very easy. For most sites your most important landing page is your home page, but you have multiple concerns that have to be addressed. We are going to help you improve how you use your home page and track its effects.

Hopefully you are ready to take on the challenge of consolidating your goals in a concise manner. The better you use your home page the clearer your visitors will understand the context in which they are interacting with you.

Who are the people who visit your site? Who are you serving? The answer is *not* **everyone**. Different stages in the buying cycle and general approaches are combative in the way they interact with your path of action. It is difficult to perfectly satisfy the people who want immediate success and the people who want lots of information in the same stroke. But there are ways to accommodate more than one mode of interaction.

Customer Types

If you have read *Waiting For Your Cat To Bark* by FutureNow, Inc. or *Landing Page Optimization* by Tim Ash, you will recognize the use of a modified Keirsey-Bates scale, separating people into four groups. There are many ways of splitting up personalities, but for the purpose of designing you will find the best value in models that are based on behavior. Because it is simple and behavioral we use similar terms as the Eisenbergs and FutureNow:

- **Relational**—people who connect through human story, driven by emotions.
- **Researcher**—people who connect through logic, driven by information.
- **Competitive**—people who connect through comparison, driven by a mix of emotion and timing.
- **Immediate**—people who connect through immediate interactions, driven by a mix of emotion and information.

Your first challenge is to think, truthfully, about whom your product is serving. If you are selling point and shoot digital cameras your customer is different than if you are selling a high-end digital SLR camera. But remember, temperaments are more of an indicator of style than need. For the travel industry the issue is more about branding than service; this may also be the case for your site.

Relational customers are the ones that care if people like a product. They are the most likely to be swayed by testimonials. Often they are concerned with ease of use and product support. You can improve your conversions with this type of user by displaying how you stand behind your products, or by telling them who you are.

Researchers are the customers who care about specs. They want to make a logical decision about a product's relative value. They are also most likely to be price conscious, because they research to find a good value. Researchers are more likely to gravitate toward things that can be researched and found to be the best option; they are the type of people who will spend a month researching before buying. You can better connect to Researchers by offering them information.

Competitive customers are the ones that are most likely to be early adopter or pre-sale customers. Why, you ask? Because they are competitive, they want to be the first to have something. They are also the customers that are most likely drawn toward high-end products—if you can't be first, be best. There are quite clearly two types of Competitive customers—those that are feature-driven and those that are benefit-driven. Improving your conversions with Competitive customers means selling brands that have social cache, or building your brand cache.

Immediate customers are driven by impulse; they are most likely to engage time-based messaging. Selling to Immediate customers is often contingent on giving them enough information to support their decision. Converting an Immediate visitor into a customer can be as simple as offering a sale. It can be difficult to convert an Immediate customer if you are offering something that they can get in a store and have today. Shipping policies and incentive programs are good ways to target Immediate customers. However, maintaining brand loyalty with this type of customer is more difficult than it is with any other temperament.

Your next question to ask is: why is this person shopping online? Each of the temperaments uses the Internet in a different way.

Researchers are very likely doing research. They are also the customers that are most concerned with features. Some Competitive customers are also looking for features. These people come looking for the information to satisfy their desires; giving them more information than your competitors is one way to build their loyalty.

Relational and some Competitive customers are more likely to know what they want. The benefits-driven Competitives purchase and interact on branding so are less likely to need additional information; they often decide because of social cues instead of concrete data. Relational customers are most likely to be doing offline research, by asking friends and family or hearing a review from a trusted source. So these people come knowing what they want and your job is to reinforce their decision.

Social context or the cache of a service/product generally drives Competitive customers. The iPhone is a good example of a product that attracts Competitive customers. However, if you ask why they have the particular product, answers will vary. Some rationalize the features, some call out benefits, and others just want to be part of the community.

Immediate customers are the most likely to browse, in part because they are generally curious people. Turning Immediate visitors into customers means inciting an immediate desire, because they are the users who will take immediate action. Focus on features and on time.

Regardless of temperament there are supporting characteristics that contribute to decisions, like a desire for process versus completion, extroversion versus introversion, or access to alternative buying channels. There are short-term motivations that have a strong effect on the exact behavior of your visitors, most often pushing them toward behaviors that are included in another general temperament (e.g. when a buying decision has been made everyone is more of an Immediate).

The temperament description is a common introduction to the concept of how people engage information. However, professional conversion optimization companies use a more complicated system—like the Meyers Briggs Types Indicator. MBTI splits each of the temperaments into four groups, for a total of 16 distinct personality types.

The basic structure of the MBTI asks the following questions:

Do you prefer focusing internally versus externally? (Extrovert or Introvert)

Do you focus on raw data or interpretation? (Intuitive or Sensing)

Do you make decisions based on logic or circumstance? (Thinking or Feeling)

Do you prefer making final decisions or leaving decisions open to change? (Judging or Perceiving)

The four Temperaments as described at Future Now:

> The Immediate ("SP"; Sensing-Perceiving)
> The Competitive ("NT"; iNtuitive-Thinking)
> The Relational ("NF"; iNtuitive-Feeling)
> The Researcher ("SJ" or Sensing-Judging)

Your type is your preference for interactions. You can read more about the types online. When you start to build a mental picture of these personalities you will get a sense for how they perform tasks differently. The hidden trap in the temperament framework is introducing context.

An example of context:

Carlos is an ENFP—Extrovert Intuitive Feeling Perceiver. But in his work life he does a lot of research and creates strategies, meaning that he spends six to eight hours per day being a Thinker. So according to the temperament system part of the day he has a Competitive approach and the rest of the day he is Relational. To complicate matters even more he was raised in a family that, for various reasons, was low-detail, meaning that results are more important than process. He rarely deviates from a Perceiving mindset; "plan for change" is one of his mottos. Consequently he often finishes his transaction process from an Immediate mode.

Since you can't pin down every individual, you want to create engagement environments that satisfy as many mindsets as possible. You never know when your visitor will switch from one buying mode to another, and they do often switch.

Do you support your visitor changing their goal? Can someone easily, with one click, switch from research to transaction? From transaction to upgrade? From testimonial to specifications?

Getting Visitors to Your Site

There are three channels that predominant marketing campaigns use for driving traffic that can influence where and how visitors find you.

- Organic search

- Online advertising: paid search, banners, paid linking
- Offline advertising

Organic search is the primary focus of search engine optimization. Gains are made by controlling your use of text, architecture, and linking to influence how search engines find and rate your content in comparison to everyone else in your space. Generally eight of ten people engage in the organic, non-paid, listings on Google™, Yahoo!®, and MSN™. There is a great deal of value in holding a high position in the organic search. But you don't control what content is shown; the search engine shows what it feels is most appropriate. So, even with diligent effort you may achieve your desired position, but with a different page of your site than intended.

Online advertising includes the advertisements and paid links that go from one site to another and the paid advertising that appears in the sponsored sections of the major search engines. Employing these links differs from using organic search because you actually get to choose where the links point. You can ensure that a clear path to action is maintained from introduction to completion.

Offline advertising is a major component in creating and securing a query space. Sometimes people don't search the way that is most beneficial for your business. Offline advertising is a clear path to shifting possible visitors toward either phrases you control, or your brand. Swaying customers toward searching your brand offers a very advantageous position where you can have maximum control over how your site is presented and certain protections against your competitors.

Note: there are plenty of other options for bringing new customers to your site, but the above mentioned are the most widely used and generally garner the most targeted traffic.

Organic Search

The Top 20 Travel Phrases By Monthly Volume (as of June 2008)

According to Google™ on phrase matching.

Keywords	Approx Avg Search Volume
hotels	226,000,000
flights	83,100,000
travel	83,100,000
travel deals	37,200,000
cheap flights	24,900,000
cheap hotels	11,100,000
vacation packages	6,120,000
air travel	1,220,000
cheap airfare	450,000
cheap travel	246,000
discount hotels	246,000
air flights	201,000

airline flights	201,000
discount travel	135,000
discount airfare	110,000
airline travel	90,500
budget travel	90,500
cheap travel deals	74,000
discount flights	49,500
cheap air travel	14,800
Total	474,648,300

Every month on Google™ the four travel aggregators fight over approximately 475 million searches for these phrases, so across all engines and including long-tail phrases there are more than 1,000,000,000 searches per month that relate to travel.

According to Google™ Trends, Compete™, and Quantcast™, Expedia® (the leader by volume) gets almost triple the traffic that Hotwire™ (the lowest) gets. Travelocity™ and Orbitz™ run neck and neck in the middle.

Compete™:

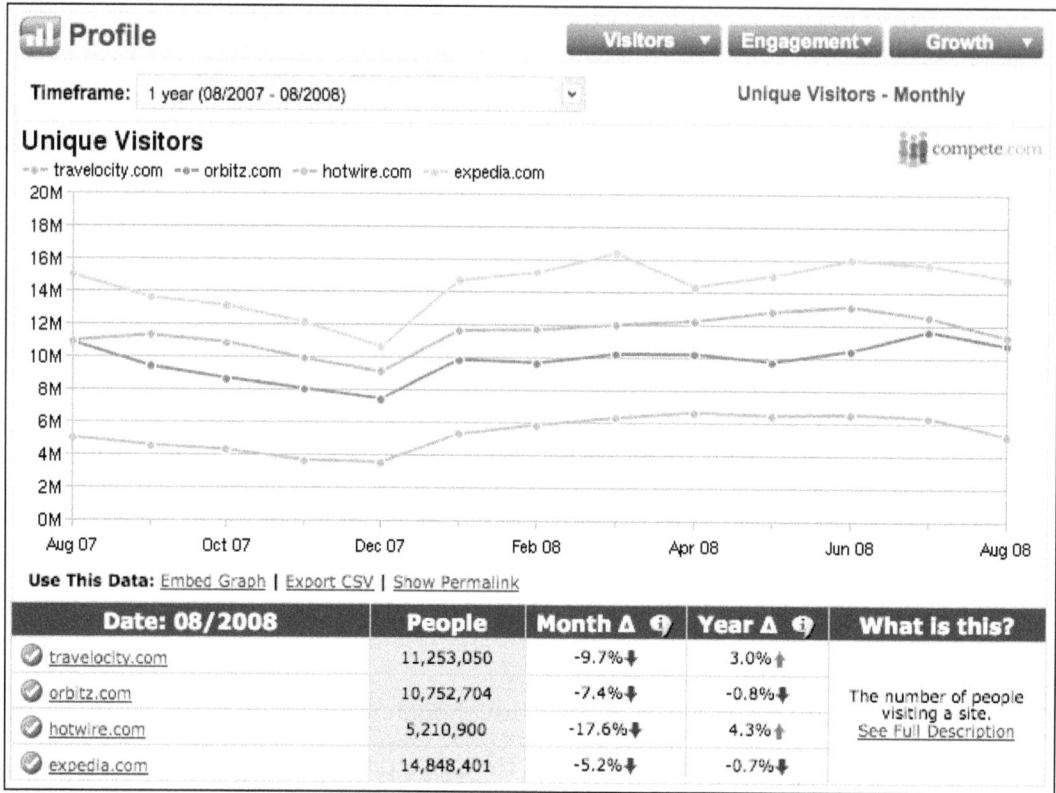

Compete™ estimates 14.8 million visitors per month for Expedia®. By conservative estimate Compete™ is probably low by at least a power of two. It is important to note that Expedia®, Hotwire™, and Hotels.com™ are partner organizations.

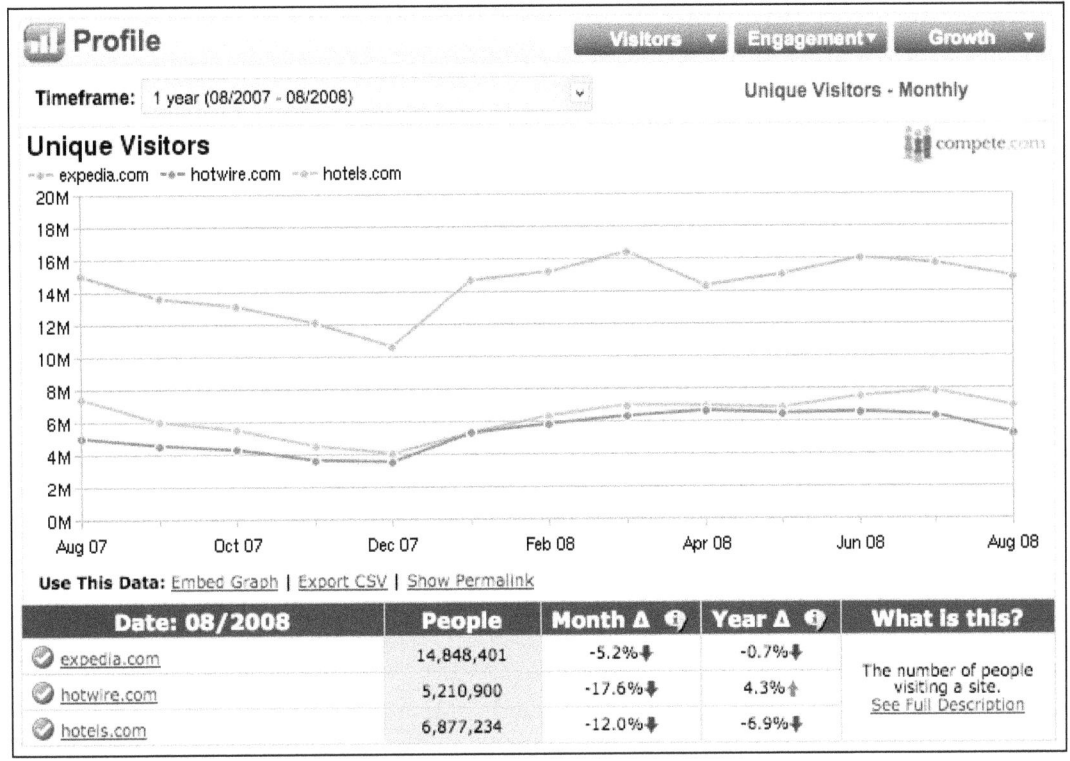
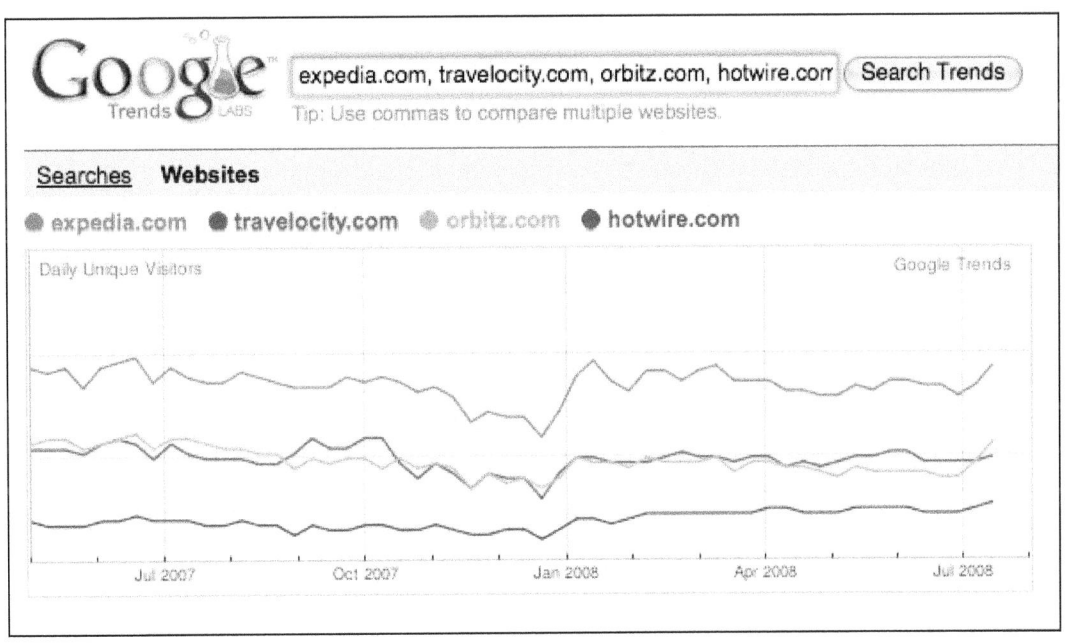

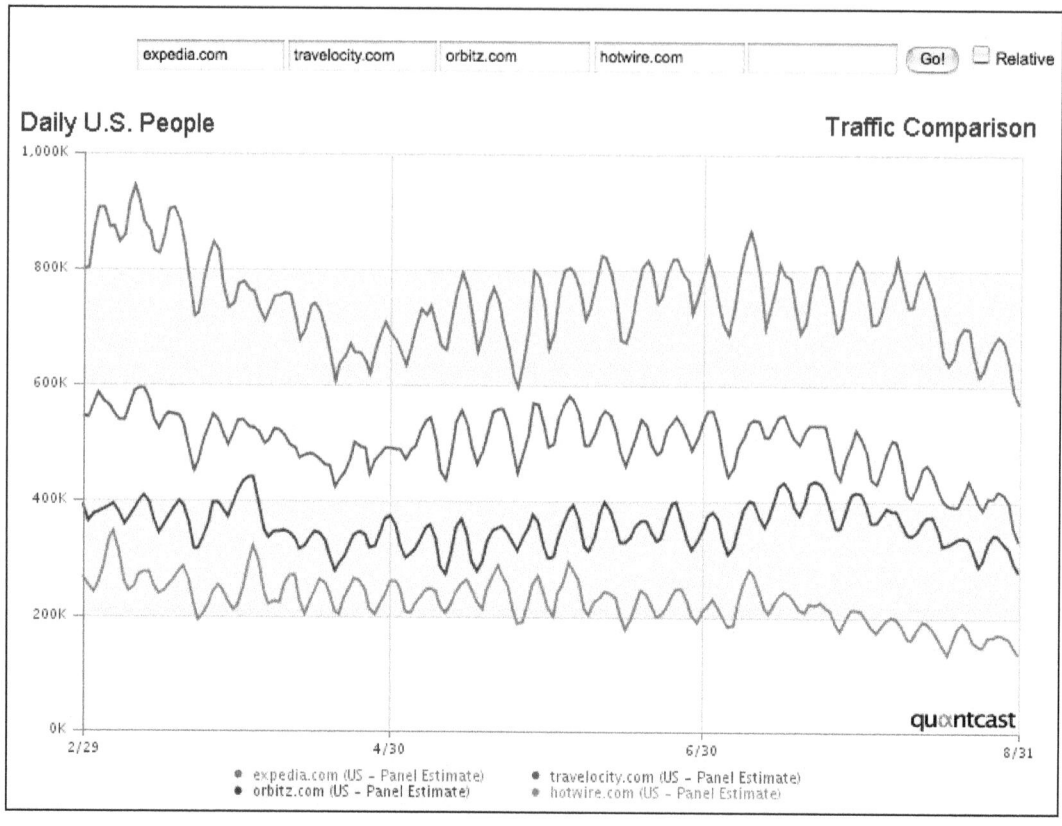

Clearly Expedia® is the traffic winner; likely their sites see more than 50 million visits per month. But that is small compared to the total market, and you have to consider how much of their traffic is based on brand.

The Importance of Paid Search

In Google™, Yahoo!®, and MSN™ , travel terms, including brand names, warrant paid search that is shown above organic search. This means regardless of any of these sites' success in making the first page, there is a degree to which the search engines will sell your business to anyone willing to pay. This is not the case for most businesses, but you should look into this when you take on your changes. Check your prized terms to see how much paid search will affect your organic successes.

The major positive of online advertising is that you can choose where you place the visitors. If you are paying to have your brand and site placed in front of potential visitors you should be taking the time to fulfill their expectations.

So how well do you back your dollars? Imagine that you are bidding on the word *hotels.* What should be included on your landing page? The word *hotels* should be highlighted in some way, any radio buttons should be checked, a picture of a *hotel* room or *hotel* room and happy people, and guarantee on *hotels* should be prominent.

Offline Advertising

Monthly Brand Searches According to Google™

Based on broad match.

Keywords	Approx Avg Search Volume
expedia	3,350,000
travelocity	2,740,000
orbitz	2,240,000
hotwire	673,000

And these numbers don't take into account type in/direct traffic numbers. None of these sites really owns organic search. As of September 2008 Orbitz™ is the only one of the four that is represented first page organically for all of the top three searched phrases on Google™ and Yahoo!®, and Orbitz™ only misses one phrase—*hotels*—on MSN™.

This makes branded search very important. Getting people to search your brand creates a clear advantage in paid placement and a best-case scenario for your organic control. Offline advertising may not be part of your online strategy, but it should be. Creating offline brand recognition can be of particular importance in attracting visitors that are Relationally or Competitively driven by creating a social value for your brand.

What to Look For in the Following Chapters

The four approaches that we are describing in this book are using the home page as a landing page and other aspects of the brand as tools for making extreme examples of catering to a customer type. We will also call out web analytics data that will help you determine the type of user your site attracts.

We use some hypothetical companies and some actual companies in the travel industry for each of our sections to maintain a common language, but these recommendations can be applied to any site. All Above the Fold and All About Speed are about reworking the visual aspects of websites. All About the Customer and All About Retention address customer acquisition and customer care issues. We suggest that you visit sites like some of the major travel sites to make some comparisons of who uses various tactics that we describe.

All Above the Fold

"A person buying ordinary products in a supermarket is in touch with his deepest emotions."
-John Kenneth Galbraith

"Few people at the beginning of the nineteenth century needed an adman to tell them what they wanted."
-John Kenneth Galbraith

John Galbraith could have easily said these things about the Internet and about web design. These two quotes address customers with an immediate need. Immediate need visitors or customers do not typically concern themselves with the extra frills found on websites. They come to a website because they know exactly what they want.

When you land on a page you have essentially the same experience as looking at a newspaper in a stand; you make an instant judgment of the content based on what you see up front. On the Internet this first impression is a screen, one screen without scrolling. One of the major positives of Google™'s search is the sparse functional design. It is a contrast to portal sites like Yahoo!® and MSN™ , which have dozens of links, ads, and other bells and whistles. Consider what travel aggregators would look like if they followed a similar model.

When you think about how the Google™ approach is different from the Yahoo!® approach and which is better for your site, consider the questions from your customer's standpoint. Do your customers come to your website with a specific item or service in mind, or are they just doing research? How are your customers reaching you? Are they directly loading your website, clicking on a targeted email, or are they finding you through search and ads? The answers to these questions will help lead you toward whether you should use a minimalist approach—All Above the Fold.

To more specifically determine whether an All Above the Fold approach is a good option for you to choose, the following data will help you answer this question. If your link click report shows that the number of clicks on the submit button of your function unit is below the amount you thought it would be or if visitors are clicking on one or more unintended or non-buying links more than they are clicking on the function unit, you might want to consider simplifying your landing page. If your page report shows that page conversion for your landing page is not what you expected or if the landing page has a high bounce rate, consider the following section as an option to help correct this problem.

We are not going to take this landing page all the way to the extreme—only function unit and nothing else. Instead we are going to take a hypothetical company—Alpha Co.—and show you how we would change their landing page from one of a typical travel aggregator to an All Above the Fold travel site.

Alpha Co. has found that while they are competitive at getting visitors to their site, their landing page conversion is not quite as good as what they expected it to be. Also, they were able to combine a pathing analysis with a link click report and top departure page report and determine that many visitors are getting to the landing page and clicking on one of their numerous Deals links, going to a Deals page, and then abandoning.

Alpha Co. is a prime candidate for the All Above the Fold approach based on their data. The current home page is more than one full screen in length (above represents their page viewed at 800 by 600 pixels), as are those of their major competitors. By making changes to their landing page, they aim for visual improvement and functional advantage over their competitors.

While many sites report lower percentages of users (about 10 percent) that have screen resolutions of 800 x 600 or less[1], to design All Above the Fold you should incorporate all users. Going back as early as 2006 people like Jakob Nielsen have been saying that designing around 1224 x 786 should be standard[2], but even Nielsen stresses the importance of 800 x 600 support.

---

[1] http://www.w3schools.com/browsers/browsers_display.asp

[2] http://www.useit.com/alertbox/screen_resolution.html

In this case study we are not discussing standard design. All Above the Fold is a specific design criteria. If you want near 100 percent execution of this concept you need to be designing less than 600 pixels vertically. The expansion of alternative smaller hardware like netbooks, mini laptops intended for Internet use, and mobile web browsing increase the importance of building well within the common dimensions if you are intent on a one-screen design.

To make the transition, Alpha Co. needs to make changes to:

- Total page layout
- Content placement
- Link presentation on the main landing page

Total Page Layout

Sites that have to serve a diverse range of customers need to present a design that can be displayed on even older computers. This means creating a website that is less than 800 pixels wide. To accomplish an All Above the Fold layout means also being less than 600 pixels tall. So, your major concern is choosing how to layout your elements.

>Function—booking a flight, cell phone update, search, and user administration
>
>Protection—price assurance
>
>Up sell—sales, packages, and credit card
>
>Long sell—rewards from the credit card

The current home page spends half of its real estate on up sell, which we feel is a bad choice for the main landing page. Alpha Co. also has a disjointed layout—a top banner surrounded by a small amount of white space, a blue left column, an orange right header, and white background for sign in, registration, and search. Seemingly unrelated pieces appear to be quilted together, giving the layout an unplanned feel.

The first step in creating an All Above the Fold home page is prioritizing your presentation. Many sites have banners at the top of the page. Remove this advertising space and get directly to the functional parts of your site, like navigation. It is a safe assumption that you need to fit inside 800 x 600 pixels to achieve one screen on almost all computers. One frequent issue we see is the use of too many background and text color combinations; this results in designs that are too frenetic to be useful.

Content Change

Based on most travel sites, the primary issue Alpha Co. needs to overcome after taming frenetic design is choosing the right content to fill a reduced space. Because the home page is the primary landing page for most sites they need to be focused on their primary business objective.

Under the proposed layout changes to the function module, travel booking will be moved to the upper left of the page. This is where it will be most visible. Next, get rid of redundant elements advertising vacation packages and deals. To apply for your credit card is more than likely not why people come to the site; they come to find travel. So here is the landing page we would make, with some explanation to follow:

Function is on the left side; long sale elements, customer service elements, search, and up sell elements are on the right. More white space around the key takeaways makes them more important in the composition of the page. Now deals and RSS are prominent, featured deals are visible, and a testimonial is paired with the point of action—finding a flight.

Things that should be tested:

- Find Flight versus Book Travel—you should test leading a visitor's immediate goal versus end goal for engagement and form completion.
- Different Color for Right Column Outline—using a different color can help draw attention from one section to another.

- Testimonial Topic—what is the major concern that a person may have in submitting? Do you get more use/completion from one long testimonial or two that cover different issues?

- Form Structure—the current form is unfocused. It can be tightened by moving the flight preference next to Number of Travelers and the submit buttons can be laid out horizontally. This will make filling in the form more intuitive.

- Get Rid of Redundant Tabs—there are a number of unnecessary tabs. The radio buttons already serve the function of changing what you are asking for. It is confusing to have that level of overlap.

- Place the Price Assurance on the Right—the current function unit is very dense. Moving the price assurance could give the flight unit a less daunting appearance. Also, the price assurance link distracts the visitor from the main goal of submitting a travel request.

Analysis

The overarching goal of the All Above the Fold concept is increasing visitor penetration into the site. By reducing choices and focusing on an immediate sense of progress you are catering to spontaneous and competitive mindsets that want to achieve results. You can expect a drastic change in what you see from your visitors by making this kind of change.

Main metrics you should use to measure: single page visits (bounces), site exits (top departure pages) or page exit ratio, visit duration, time spent on-page, page views per visit, frequency of function unit submits, visitor to buyer path completion, clickstream report and, most importantly, site conversion.

Disclaimer

Please keep in mind that any major change, even a positive one, will scare some users. It is important to pair these results with other metrics and not evaluate success or failure by just one metric.

Technical Properties Report

If your analytics provider collects information based on JavaScript tagging, you should make use of a technical properties tag for your landing page (if offered). Technical properties tags tell the analytics provider to collect information like customer/email id, browser type, display settings, monitor size, etc. If your analytics provider collects information based on log files, you should investigate whether this information can be gathered from the log files. The technical properties of your visitors are of special importance when you are considering design changes for your landing page.

For All Above the Fold, it is especially important to monitor your browser types, monitor resolution, and screen size reports in the technical properties section of you web ananlytics. These reports will give you insight into your customer. You can segment out conversion and function unit submits by these different types of visitors to find out if your landing page improvement needs to focus on a specific browser type or ensure that your changes look nice in your visitors' screen resolutions.

Single Page Visits (Bounces)

What this metric will tell you: of the people who entered your site via the landing page in question, how many exited the site upon viewing the page and took no further action on your site?

What does bounce rate mean? First, you should have a comparison number for old versus new and a site-wide average for all entry pages, or a number that you feel is an acceptable amount of traffic leaving the site. Generally speaking, you want your new landing page to have a lower bounce rate than the previous landing page and site-wide average; however, this is a delicate issue. Any major change, even a positive one, will scare some people. Consequently, it is especially important to pair bounce rate with another metric.

Possible pairings include:

- Bounce Rate versus Beginning the Completion Path from Home Page—if your visitors are segmenting into users and non-users more distinctly this may be a win.

- Bounce Rate versus Pages per Visit—if you are separating into engaged versus non-engaged visitors this can also lead to positive information.

- Bounce Rate versus Site Abandonment—look to see three things: do users have higher loyalty, do users more often engage secondary conversions, or do users exit differently.

- Bounce Rate versus Site-Wide Conversion—if bounce rate is higher than previous data but site-wide conversion is up, this just means that you were successful at weeding out those customers who were not going to make a purchase in the first place.

Finally, while we recommend that you compare your data to a prior time frame (such as last month, last quarter or last year) to gauge whether you have improved your numbers, you must keep in mind that sometimes seasonal changes or outside factors such as the economy may influence your results and may not be comparable to the prior year. A great example of this is in the travel industry, where there is a strong connection to fuel prices. Don't take for granted that lower engagement is a result of your content. There may be user factors that are more responsible for your change in use.

Site Exits (top departure pages)

Considering the average site conversion is 2.5 percent, it is an understatement to say that the majority of your visitors are doing something other than buying on your website. So what are they doing? One way to answer this is to find out where they are departing. You know that some percentage of your visitors is not clicking on the submit button, so what were they looking at? Top departure pages can tell you several things such as what your top departed pages are and whether they are pages you expected to be top departing.

You should begin your process with the pages that have the highest number of exits and follow with the pages with the highest percentage of exits. If your landing page is your top departing page (often this is the case) then this recommendation or one of our other recommended changes can help to lower your departure rate. Be aware that your top trafficked page may continue to be the top departed page even after a change is made, so you should focus on whether there was a decrease in your performance metrics, raw number or percentage.

Because you have significantly changed the access to information, you should change your approach to information. In the case of e-commerce or anything that has customer service you should set points within the customer service process that are considered natural satisfaction points.

Visitors exiting from customer service contact or FAQ pages are very important to your business. If they are getting customer service numbers and calling they should be considered served; if you are not getting comparable contact volume to visits you have a red flag. You can get some very valuable information about your website by considering how it engages offline interactions.

Help pages are meant to answer questions without the assistance of phone/email contact. The changes to Alpha Co. significantly lower the barrier to help and customer service sections. Large volumes of traffic passing from Help to Contact means your web content is dissatisfying, or lacking. High exits from Help sections can also be a red flag. Consider partitioning your Help section based on content that is expected to answer a question not related to continuation of visit and information that is generally part of a completion process that should continue.

In the example of travel, checking information on travel insurance is probably occurring during the decision-making process. Cancellation policy is ambiguous, so it should include a link to the effect of *Do You Need to Cancel a Reservation?* This way you can segment the people who are at a natural satisfaction point.

In total you are looking for a decrease in abandonment mid-process and a shift toward satisfaction points—regardless of the end point.

An alternative measurement to this metric is page exit rate, which compares the number of times a visitor exited the site via a page in question divided by the total number of times the page was viewed. Unless the page in question is a typical departure page, such as an order confirmation-page or a help page, you want a fairly low page exit rate, approximately in the 10-15 percent range.

Visit Duration

While fairly self explanatory, visit duration can tell you some very interesting things about your customer. If your average time on-site jumps from two minutes to four minutes this can be good or bad. If you see a correlating spike in orders, then you know that the change made to your landing page was more successful at driving your visitors forward through your website. However, it could also mean that what was once an easy process from start to finish is now an elongated process due to the changes you made. You should correlate this metric with orders/conversion, and if these metrics also go down then you know the changes that you made were not positive.

In addition to visit duration, you should measure time spent on-page in several ways. First, if you see a dramatic change in time on-site find out if your most popular pages have a high time on-page. If your popular pages have high time on-page this could mean that they are either highly engaged with these pages or they are getting stuck on these pages and are not sure where to go next. Check these pages for page abandonment. Also, be sure to review the page yourself and ask, Is there a lot of unnecessary content to read that would cause time on-page to be higher than other pages? Remember, in this scenario your first goal is conversion, second goal is subscription, and third goal is retention. So you may want certain pages to have high time on-page. However, you may not want these pages on your main path to checkout.

In the case of landing pages, keep in mind that typically these are not included in visit duration due to the nature of calculation (see glossary for more details).

Finally, be sure to check for a correlation between time on-site and phone volume. If your phone volume increases you are either better transporting visitors to interaction, or you have introduced an issue that requires human interaction. Take advantage of the contact to get information from your users.

Pages per Visit and Page Views

The bottom line is booking. Successful changes should move you pages per visit closer to the number of pages required to complete a transaction. If you begin with average pages that are less than your completion track (e.g. sale, lead, etc.) then you want to see pages increase along with percentage of views to your completion track pages. If you started with a higher average then your completion process you should be paying attention to the pages that are increasing in visits. Where you see increased traffic are the sections of your site that your visitors were searching for prior to your uncluttering.

You will want to pay special attention to improving these pages as a second round of revisions. Any page that is outside your completion path that sees noticeable increase is a possible bottleneck to your completion, or contains particularly valuable information. Look into what your visitors are asking you to expand by creating additional value in areas they expand into.

Frequency of Function Unit Submits

This will give you a different number than page conversion. This should come from the number of submits divided by the total number of unique visits (sessions) and will help to find out if making the function unit more prominent leads to more submits. If it does, then obviously you have achieved your main goal (and this should be your main goal). If this number goes down, you should verify whether page abandonment has gone up. Also check your page conversion and site conversion. If conversion is down, submits are down, and abandonment is up then you can determine that this method is not right for your landing page.

If you don't already track submit to unique visit rate, you can find this data by either adding a click event tag on the submit button, or with certain services that use specialty tags like form tags, event tags, element tags, etc. This will probably give you a number specific to how many unique submits versus unique visits your page produces. If you are receiving submits in a number that suggests multiple submits per user you need to establish why. Possible process issues that cause multiple submits include technical problems and browser users. If you are getting many requests from your visitors it means that you either are not fulfilling their needs on some level or you have an opportunity to capitalize on a buying behavior.

High submit to total conversions should be a point of great attention. If you are attracting the browsing/researching type of visitors it is important to consider very specific measures to increase that particular group's satisfaction and consider retention-based changes. Researchers tend not to be at decision point; you need to either help them to that point or solidify loyalty before they reach the point of action.

If your users aren't displaying research behavior then high submit to conversion is a red flag for a broken transaction process. In e-commerce terms the problem indicator would be cart abandonment. If the changes you are making have put users in your sales funnel but they aren't closing then you have a clear indicator that something in your funnel may be the barrier to conversion.

Visitor to Buyer Path Entrance (Conversion Starts)

Hopefully, you currently track your visitor to buyer path completion, or at least have this path set up in your analytics tool. Typically what this report shows you are how many unique visits you had to your site, how many browsed your product, how many added something to their carts, and how many bought something during their sessions. This may also be called funnel analysis. This is a great way to measure if there is a particular area that is underperforming, or is causing a blockage to the final order. It also gives you a more in depth view of step-by-step completion of the conversion process.

If you have 1,000 visitors, and only 500 make it to a product/browse page, you have to ask yourself where 50 percent of your initial visitors are moving to. Also, if after redesign you see this number increase, then obviously your landing page is working better at driving visitors to the buying process. If this number drops, first check to see if overall conversion has dropped as well. If it has then you can also check page abandonment and time on-site. If abandonment is up and time on-site is down it is safe to say that this option for a landing page is not appealing to your customer. If abandonment is up and time on-site is also up, it could either mean that visitors are not sure of what to do next, or are possibly getting side tracked with something on a particular page. If abandonment is the same or down but time on-site is up, it could mean that something about the page is distracting visitors and keeping them from moving forward in the process, so further changes may need to be made.

Finally, let's say prior to redesign 1,000 visitors came to your landing page and 600 went on to a browse page, 200 added to cart, and 25 made a purchase; after redesign 1,000 visitors came to your landing page, 700 went on to a browse page, 200 added to cart, and 25 made a purchase. If you only looked at conversion, you wouldn't see a positive change in overall conversion, so you would possibly be disappointed and might make the mistake of deciding that your landing page changes aren't working; you might revert back. The pathing report actually shows you that your landing page was more successful at driving visitors forward in the process, however only the same number added to cart and purchased. What this means is that you need to look at the rest of the process. However, that is not going to be addressed in this text. It could possibly mean your conversion is maxed at 2.5 percent, or maybe it's just not the right season for you. Possibly, you may need to review your product set to see if you are offering a competitive product.

Click Paths Report

Click path reporting shows you where your visitors go after viewing a particular page. Typically you would set this up prior to pathing analysis to determine what the main path is through your site. The main difference in this report versus pathing analysis is that you have less control over the steps and the conversions. This report is great at telling you what the most traveled route through your site is. It also shows you secondary and tertiary nuances of what people are viewing on your site. On each step you get multiple ideas of what the top clicked and viewed areas are.

This is where your exit and site abandonment numbers become valuable. Pair the common paths to common exit pages, especially when they are close to your average page views. In the same manner, you should follow your common paths to completion.

Site Conversion

Site conversion is a widely used performance indicator because this metric gives you a bare bones assessment of whether your site is successful at generating a lead or getting an order (or whatever else is the intent of your site). Conversion rate as a metric is typically used as the safety net for other metrics. While site conversion is a great bar to evaluate your site, it doesn't ever tell the entire story, and thus other metrics should be used in conjunction with it.

Understanding why people convert is more important than the number of completions. Looking into the supporting parts, such as clickpath and exits, will tell you more about why you are making conversions than the conversion rate will tell you.

Now What?

Depending on the volume of traffic that your site incurs, as well as the length of your buying process, you will want to collect enough data to make an informed decision on whether your changes have corrected your issues. The amount of data that you collect post-change should equal the amount of data used to inform the change. You should compare the pre-data to the post-data to see where your wins are and to inform what changes might still need to be made. If you do not see lift from the actions that are taken in this method you should be asking what mode of interaction needs to be addressed. In particular this design, All Above the Fold, leaves out those people who are driven human connections and doesn't strongly address the needs of researchers.

Certain signals like submits to unique visitor, use of Help and FAQ documents, and contact volume are flags that suggest your next steps should involve testing elements that are more relational or more customer attentive. These types of changes are highlighted in our reviews of All About the Customer and All About Retention. If you see a conversion improvement in your visitors with larger screen resolution, you can confirm that this change is positive for your site. If you see your bounce rate increase and conversion drop, you can confirm that this is not a positive change for your site. With proper user testing prior to launch you should know whether or not to expect a bounce rate increase.

All About Speed

"A lot of people run a race to see who is fastest. I run to see who has the most guts, who can punish himself into exhausting pace, and then at the end, punish himself even more."
Steve Prefontaine

In All Above The Fold we reduced certain elements that had a derivative effect on driving visitors toward the main goal—utilizing the function unit. Additionally, we attempted to create a site where all features would be shown above the fold. While this in itself should help increase the speed of the site and decrease page load time, there is more that you can do.

As computers and Internet speeds have improved, websites have expanded to take advantage. Many sites have taken the approach of using flashier presentation to stand out from their competitors. According to websiteoptimization.com average page size has tripled since 2003 from 94k to 312k. The number of objects on a page has doubled in that same time frame, from 25.7 to 49.9.[1]

The result is very obvious in the travel industry where lush photos of tropical places entice visitors to dream about lavish vacations. But, large banners and Flash rollovers create long load times for the bulk of users and leave little room for the information that most users want. A study comparing February 2006 to February 2008 by Keynote™ shows that while narrowband connections have felt the impact of larger page size and additional objects, broadband connections have increased with the pace of page size, so page

---

[1] www.websiteoptimization.com/speed/tweak/evolution-web/

load time has actually decreased since 2006.[1] Most businesses operate off of a T1 line which is classified as medium speed, but depending on the amount of users on the T1 line, download times can be as slow as a narrowband (dial up) connection. Generally speaking, broadband connection is not in the majority. Exact statistics are hard to come by regarding what percent of Internet users in the United States have broadband. There are plenty of statistics on home use, but due to the high use of the Internet at work, it may be hard to get a true count of exact penetration. So, while it is good to prepare your website for a medium to high speed connected visitor, you should know and be comfortable with the download time that it takes for a narrowband visitor to load your page. In addition, according to the website fatpipe.com, global penetration of broadband is 20 percent as of January 2008.[1] So if your potential customer base includes traffic from outside the U.S., you should ensure that your website loads quickly on a narrowband connection.

If your site is very content-heavy and takes a long time to load on any of the connection speeds, you should analyze bounce rate data and segment out each connection category. This will tell you if your site is too content-rich for a dial up connection. If the majority of your visitors use a dial up/narrowband connection, then this section will give you an insightful idea for correcting this issue. If through your link analysis you determine that the click through rate of your function unit is below your expectations, this section will help inspire your decision for change. Finally, if you determine from your path completion report or funnel report that the number of visitors that move from the landing page to the next step is below your

---

[1] http://www.websiteoptimization.com/speed/tweak/average-web-page/

expectations, this section will assist you in developing and making a meaningful change to your website.

So as a next step, or as an alternative, this chapter discusses the All About Speed approach. How do you create a fast-acting website both from a functional standpoint and from connection speed standpoint? Minimalist websites—Google™ or Domjax.com (a domain checking tool)—have a certain appeal in the modern web. Stripping away all bells and whistles guarantees that no matter how slow the users' connection they can achieve a fast loading landing page. To accomplish this you must take the concepts from All Above the Fold and apply a critical eye and reduce all graphic elements to achieve minimal impact.

It is important to know that clean and simple does not mean empty. If you are going for speed and professional appearance there will still be some need for graphics to offer a comfortable experience that is efficient. For instance, even though Google™'s home page is very simplistic the logo is memorable and the function unit is prominent. Additionally, the font used for the limited text that is on the site is a very traditional text (Times New Roman) and is an acceptable font that is neither too small nor too large for the visitor to see. In addition to the function unit and the logo, Google utilizes a top navigation for advanced or returning users that offers additional services. So, even though Google offers a very minimalist approach to their landing page they still offer flexibility to their users.

Imagine Beta Co. is a minimalist site that surpasses even our Alpha Co. design for immediate gratification. They followed these steps:

---

[1] http://www.fatpipeonline.com/departments.php?department_id=12&article_id=399

Reduce home page to four elements:

- Basic top navigation with logo
- Function unit
- Awards/Testimonials (JD Power™, consumer reports, etc.)
- Sitemap

It would look like this.

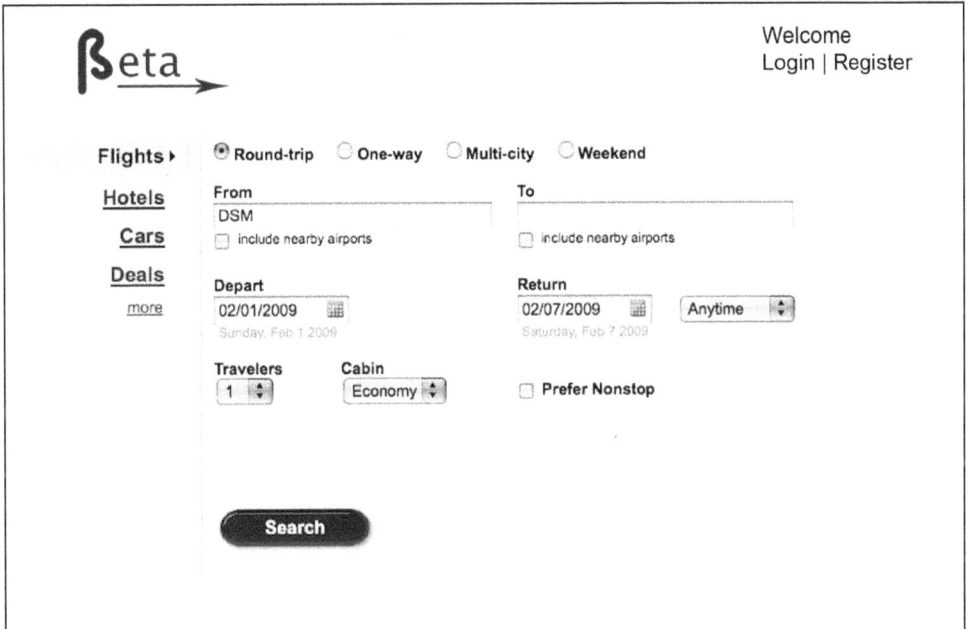

- Remove all images other than function unit, logo, top navigation, and award graphics. This reduces the total bytes of images and the total number of objects.
- Change JavaScript rollover to CSS rollover. Calling multiple scripts can cause a noticeable increase in total load time.

- Reduce scripting—some functions require the use of scripting, but if you can find an opportunity to leave a script out you should take it.

According to a 2008 Pew Internet and American Life Project poll, 55 percent of all adult Americans have home broadband connections[1]. So the other 45 percent have something else such as a 56K or a medium band connection. Prognosticators in 2004 stated that broadband penetration would be much higher than it actually is right now. As a result many companies ensure that their site runs smoothly on a broadband connection, but do not test the slower connection speeds. We recommend the opposite—test your site on the slowest connection speed to ensure that all users can access your site in a reasonable timeframe.

The travel aggregators we talked about in the introduction range from 211kb to 587kb; Beta Co.'s goal is to be just under 100kb. At T1 speeds, what people likely have or beat at work, this reduces the load time to 2.5 seconds.

So for those with a slower connection speed (56K users), the size reduction drops load time from 42 seconds (the smallest site) to 19 seconds. This also creates a site that is easy to use at 3G, for modern cell phones, and works both as a standard page and as a single column.

The actual process to get from landing page to function unit to results should be decreased. Time on-page for the landing page should have a fairly dramatic drop depending on what it was prior to redesign.

One of the biggest factors in creating a fast loading site is actually the number of elements, not the size of the elements. Because it takes time for

---

[1] www.pewinternet.org/PPF/r/305/press_release.asp

the browser and server to communicate—an average of two seconds per object—removing every object you can gives you better efficiency. At the time of publishing, Hotwire™.com, for example, has 128 object requests, meaning over 20 seconds of their load time on a T1 line are the result of latency. Even minimizing the number of images that are called can make the difference you need to be the fastest site in your industry.

Reducing the load time of the site has an additional positive side effect that we address more in "All About the Long Sell;" a faster website should also mean faster mobile web. If you create a fast operating site, with minimal options, your mobile web application should also be very easy to use. There are many initiatives right now for improving the mobile web. The biggest movement is to streamline mobile web with the Internet. It's called the One Web Principle.[1]

At present a cell phone running on 3G networks will transfer information at 128kb/s–700 kb/s on average depending on the equipment and environmental factors like travel speed and interference. The Beta Co. of today would take between 10 to 19 seconds to load on a phone. Under the proscribed changes a cell phone running under optimal condition would download the Beta homepage in four to nine seconds.

Reducing the JavaScript and image load of the page as described below will make using Beta Co. on a phone faster than using Expedia®, the most bandwidth intensive site (currently 587Kb), on a T1 line. As a unique value that is enormous. Being able to serve desktop speeds to a cell phone would

---

[1] http://www.staygolinks.com/the-multi-web-practice
http://www.w3.org/Mobile/

make anyone a winner in the currently growing culture of iPhone™ and Blackberry™. All changes that we describe on Beta Co.'s site serve to enhance the current branding of tech/budget savvy, serving the mass of driven users that are more impressed by function over research.

Things that should be tested:

- Size of Testimonial Graphics—discover the difference between using high attention graphics of value versus smaller graphics that function as accessories to the main content.

- Inclusion of Testimonial—discover whether users are more swayed by why you are an award winner. The high-speed design does not provide a high human feel; a small concession of direction may make a huge difference in initial use.

- Color of Function Unit—the difference between a large testimonial graphic and small one may be of no net effect if the user desires both reassurance and more attention pull from the function unit. If you see minimal results from changing your graphics try a more radical change.

- Use of Headline—in a very lean design your call to action at the top of the page takes on a huge amount of leverage.

- Search Box—savvy users want speed; many consider using search faster than using the sitemap. Try adding a search box to increase engagement.

- Floating feedback—much like a search box, floating feedback can give the impression of greater support and speed of use on a site.

Analysis

The overarching goal of the All About Speed concept is increasing visitor site completion and variety of use. By reducing choices and focusing on an immediate sense of progress you are catering to spontaneous and competitive mindsets that want to achieve results. You can expect a drastic change in what you see from your visitors by making this kind of change. Beyond the goals that surfaced in "All Above the Fold" you are also looking for an expansion of browser type, browser configuration, and completed page calls. So, analysis for this section calls for the following metrics: technical properties reports (connection speed/browser type/mobile users), single page visits (bounce rate), time on-page/on-site, function unit submits, click path analysis, page views/visits, page exits, and conversion.

Disclaimer

Please keep in mind that any major change, even a positive one, will scare some people. It is important to pair these results with other metrics and not evaluate success or failure by just one metric.

Technical Properties

In this case, you should monitor connection speed of your browsers, browser type, and percent of mobile web browsers. You should also consider segmenting your site-wide conversion and function units submits by connection speed, browser type, and mobile web. If conversion and function unit submits are lower for the slower connection speeds then this landing page solution might resolve this issue. If all segments' metrics appear even then you should consider one of the other sections for your landing page changes. Keep in mind that even a small positive change in conversion could equate to a large amount of profit, depending on your traffic volumes.

Single Page Visits (Bounces)

As with All Above the Fold, bounce rate will tell you whether your visitors understand and approve of your landing page. In your reporting you should have a segmentation of new visitors and repeat visitors for most reports and metrics. If bounce rate for new visitors is higher than for repeat visitors prior to redesign and after redesign, new visitors stays steady and repeat visitors spike, this landing page setup is not adequate for your visitor base. However, if both new and repeat visitors decrease in bounce rate, you should consider this an effective landing page setup as long as other key metrics improve. Finally, if new visitor bounce rate increases but repeats stay steady, this shows that your current customer base is not opposed to this change. However, the downside is that these results show your new design is not helping to encourage new visitors through the shopping process. Even more than the All Above the Fold concept, the proposed changes in All About Speed may alienate research minded or relationship-driven users. As such, bounce rate will give you a much clearer picture of how the page is performing than overall site conversion.

Many sites use Flash to create functionality/serve data in a quick way. This can greatly complicate the use of bounce rate as a metric. If your solution for speed is condensing your site function with Flash you need to take the extra time to create tagging and virtual clicks for your Flash events. If you are not creating such tags you run the risk of false bounce rates because your analytics system might not recognize actions occurring within Flash. A possible solution includes adding a time-on-page variable that negates your bounce rate assessment.

As stated above, you should not judge success or failure of your redesign (or design) based on individual metrics; rather you should pair these metrics with one another. So, in addition to segmenting bounce rate out by new versus repeat visitors, possible pairings include:

- Bounce Rate versus beginning the completion path from home page—if your visitors are segmenting into users and non-users more distinctly this may be a win.
- Bounce Rate versus pages per visit—if you are separating visitors into engaged versus leaving this can also lead to positive information.
- Bounce Rate versus site abandonment—look to see two things: do users have higher loyalty or do users exit differently.
- Bounce Rate versus site wide conversion – if bounce rate is higher than previous data but site wide conversion is up, this just means that you were successful at weeding out those customers who were not going to make a purchase in the first place.

Time On-page/On-site

Most likely you want a reduced time on-page and on-site. If this design satisfies your visitor they should be clicking through to filling out the form shortly after landing. The new design will cause an immediate change of navigation. Visitors have only four choices: top navigation, enter funnel, visit sitemap, or visit testimonial.

The real answer to what is a good change in time on-site will have to be determined by pairing this metric with something else:

- Time on-site and percentage of people who start the intended action—if you have a rising, or stagnant, time on-site, this may be an indicator of a failure in your action path. Anyone acting outside of the main function of your site should be fulfilled by your sitemap. This design is dependent upon superior communication and architecture on your sitemap.

- Time on-site and top exit page—you are looking for an increase in completions. If you are moving your exit further into your funnel you are on the right track. All About Speed also requires very straightforward help.

- Time on-site and phone volume—if your phone volume increases you have likely made a mistake in implementation. A minimalist design can be taken too far; if you have stripped necessary information, your Help use and customer service volume will be increased. Your site speed will be a pyrrhic victory if people have to call to solve usage issues.

Function Unit Submits

Without having access to your competitors' data, it's hard to know whether the rate of function unit submits is adequate. However, you should use your gut to determine whether the ratio of submits to unique visits is better or worse than your competition. An increase in this ratio is a good sign that this design is an improvement as long as no other factor, such as change in season, has an impact on your numbers. A decrease in this ratio is a sign that the new design may not be the best approach.

However, again use the new versus repeat visitor segment to determine if one segment has a marked improvement. You can also use the new versus repeat metric even if you see an increase in conversion, to know whether you are having a more positive impact on new or repeat visitors. Another factor to segment on is paid versus organic versus direct navigation traffic. All of these segments will give you a clearer understanding of how the new design affects visitors to your site. Function unit submit rate will give you a more accurate measurement of how successful the new page design is at driving visitors toward the next step.

The difference between All About Speed and All Above the Fold is that you are making almost no concessions in your included elements. Of the design methods presented in this book, this should be the most centered on action. You should expect to see a remarkable parity of submits to visitors.

Click Path Analysis

By reducing the amount of content and the number of clickable links, you have created a more direct route for visitors to follow. You have given visitors less opportunity to go elsewhere in the shopping funnel. Thus, a click path analysis is not going to be necessary. Because of the limited number of options, you can create a click path analysis that will show the step completion rate of visitors from the landing page who move to the next step of viewing prices, and then those that move on to the booking page, and then forward through the checkout process. Pathing analysis ties everything together and gives you an overall picture of the success rate of visitors through the shopping process. This will show you whether visitors drop off of the site completely or go elsewhere in the site and not on your intended path. If there is a large drop from one step to another but not a corresponding amount of site departures, a click path analysis will tell you to what other areas the visitor is going.

Because you are putting so much intent on the action path and very restricted options from the landing page, you should consider tracking the off-path sections of your site as a separate entity—perhaps going as far as making them a sub-domain that is tracked separately. This will allow you see the interaction of your major sections as referring domains—saving you time when doing analysis.

If you do take the step to build a sub-domain, consider implementing a simplified function unit that is persistent on the site. Create a separate funnel tag for submits that originate from an off-path section of the site. The location of off-path submits will highlight what your users are finding to be obstacles to completing or starting your service.

Pages per Visit and Page Views

The bottom line is booking business. Successful changes should move your pages per visit closer to the number of pages required to complete a transaction. If you begin with average pages that are less than your completion track (e.g. sale, lead, etc.), you want to see pages increase along with percentage of views to your completion track pages. If you started with a higher average, your completion process you should be paying attention to the pages that are increasing in visits. Anyone who immediately visits your sitemap should have a very low page view, or a completion.

You will want to pay special attention to improving your sitemap. Splitting the traffic so severely creates a pool of particularly valuable information. Look into what your visitors are asking you to expand by creating additional value in areas they click on this directory page.

Site Exits

If you are attempting minimalism, site exits are a critical metric. In a minimalist design the difference between great and broken is very small. All About Speed is so tailored to success-driven/action-driven users that any failure in communication can be devastating.

If you notice any spikes in site exits you MUST respond quickly. A breakdown in a popular path can have a lasting negative effect on your visitor loyalty when your visitors have a decidedly short attention span.

Site Conversion

Site conversion will tie everything together and tell you whether your changes have led more visitors to become buyers. If this metric increases and no other factor (such as seasonality) has had an impact, you can view your changes as a success. If there is a decrease, look into your segmentation. Did your repeat visitors' conversion drop or did your new visitors' conversion drop? It's more important to be sure that your repeat visitor conversion stays the same or increases; however, in order to continue increasing your customer base you will want your new visitor conversion to increase eventually as well. Again, also investigate paid marketing campaigns versus organic and direct navigation traffic.

Now What?

All About Speed is probably a radical change to your design. This means that you could see a large swing one direction or another. It is important that you commit a reasonable time frame in advance for the post analysis. Sometimes it is painful to sit through the initial response to your changes, but collecting enough information will help you make better decisions in future rounds of changes.

Lay out specific goals that you are going to track and set your conditions for closure before you start. Pay special attention to click paths that emerge from your new landing page and where your longest time on-page is occurring. Pay attention to your segmented data and whether the visitors with slower connection speeds are showing an improvement in conversion. You will want to temper this by ensuring that your overall conversion does not suffer because you've catered to a specific portion of your customers. If bounce rate or site exits increase you can confirm that this change is not good for your landing page.

A Minimal Site Requires Maximal Competency

One of the most important considerations in creating a minimalist site is maintaining a very skilled and efficient web production team. Because a design that is too minimal will essentially end interaction with visitors that are not interested in searching for answers, you must have a plan in place to provide immediate value without immediate change.

This means making page-level changes very quickly. Site-level changes should be attainable in a week if necessary. Having a very skilled writer on your team will be invaluable; headlines and FAQ communications will be your greatest strength and are essential to holding onto a user base that has a short attention span.

To capitalize on the behaviors of success-driven users, you need to create outlets for interaction that make your FAQ page unnecessary. This means being forward thinking about live chat, mobile (cell phone) interactions, and customer service. The end goal is to have a landing to completion time that clearly outclasses your competitors. If this means instant message chat or phone interactions, you should embrace these changes. Your first step is getting people into your funnel; the next is creating an almost constant sense of accomplishment that results in a very clear trail to completion.

Your loyalty will revolve around the visitors feeling that leaving you is not worth the effort of learning a different system. Once a person is a returning customer, offer them the ability to circumvent some portion of the process, but do not require them to give up attention. This means never requiring login. That's right. If you want to be perceived as the fastest option it means never interrupting your visitors with logins. Giving the option and a clear pay off helps increase loyalty, but requirements create perceived inconvenience.

Next, if you have forms that must be filled out, take the time to maintain form inputs after a refresh or a back button from an error; a huge amount of time is lost in refilling fields and the perception of loss is far worse than the actual time.

It is very important to stress that minimal design is very different from minimal information—it means reducing visual distractions.

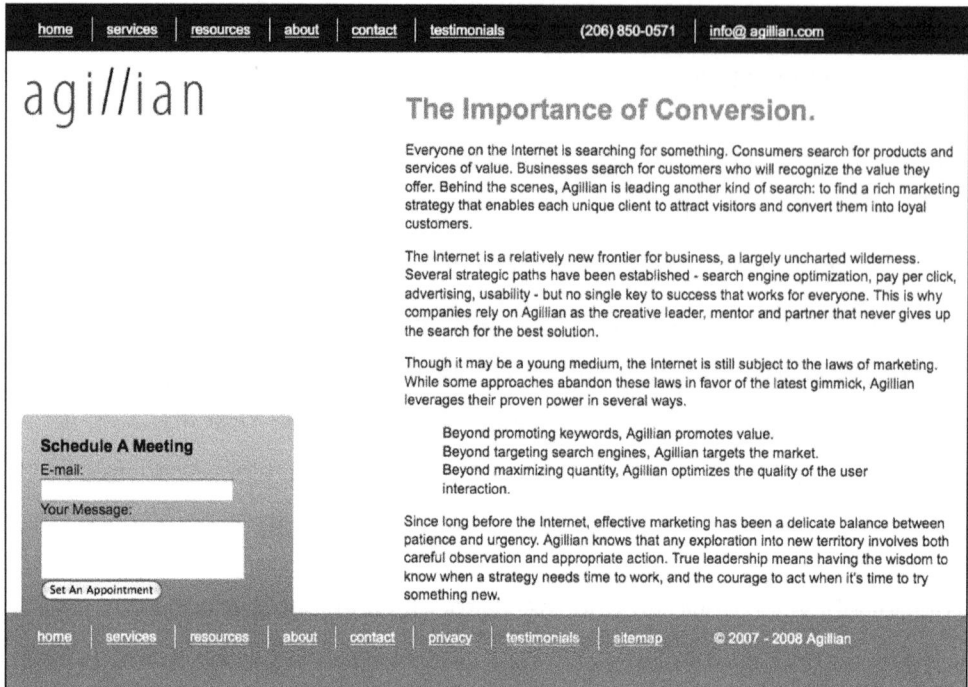

There is plenty of space in this design, which creates little distraction from the intended message. It very clearly makes the text important. Using a bold, simple palette is one of the easiest ways to establish a clear hierarchy in your content.

On the opposite end of the spectrum are portal sites like MSN™ :

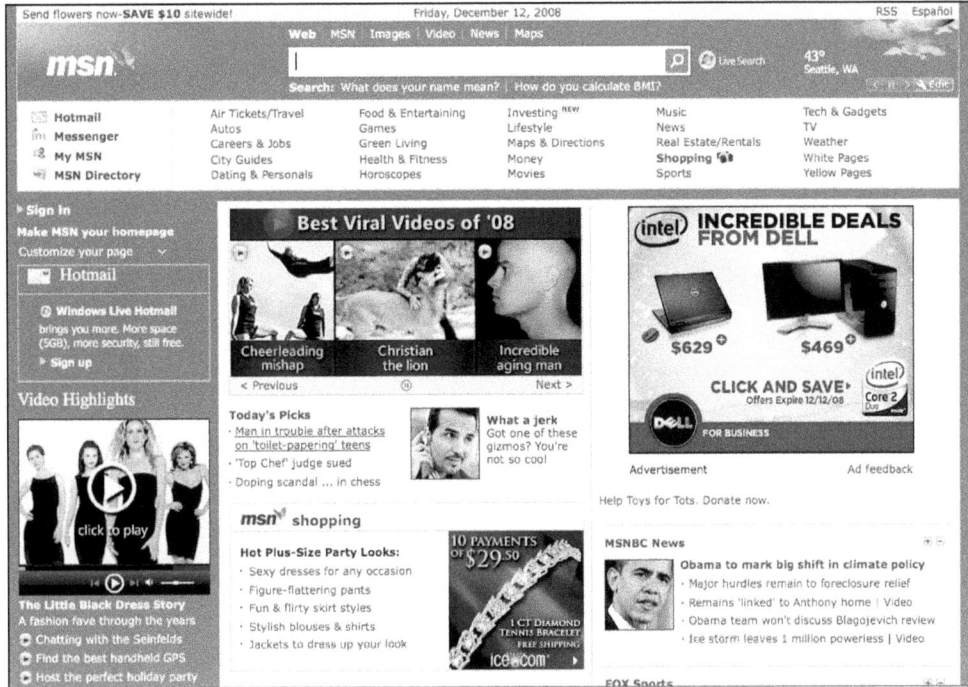

What is the most important action on the page? The MSN™ homepage above is two full screens tall and contains over 185 links. All of the text and links are the same color as the background of the design.

The idea of reducing all elements to increase speed is the basis of creating a site that has low attention needs and is easy to navigate. But, if you take the concept to its extreme you get a site like the following:

Stunning, simple, and utterly confusing. What would you do with this? Do you click? Do you move your mouse around? Do you just wait to see what happens?

A common issue with attempting minimal web design is the use of Flash. It is easy to create a design like the one above in Flash, but if that means a greater load time, that is counterproductive. When you build a site entirely in Flash you will introduce a whole new set of analytics and search-related issues. It is a safe assumption that a visitor will be JavaScript capable, but Flash is not supported by default.

All About the Customer

"If we don't take care of our customers, someone else will"

– Unknown

"If you make customers unhappy in the physical world, they might each tell 6 friends. If you make customers unhappy in the Internet, they can each tell 6,000 friends."

– Jeff Bezos

For some, the All Above the Fold and All About Speed approaches are too radical. They may just not fit with your website or business style. All About the Customer takes a very different approach while still incorporating some of the aspects of the previous two chapters. As Internet users continue to become accustomed to expansive navigation techniques, adding content to your site is becoming less likely to distract the visitors; however, it may still reduce their ability to move forward in the buying process. You want to be careful with the amount and type of content that you add. You cannot take for granted that all customers wlll enjoy a cool feature or gadget on your site.

As a web designer it can be difficult to think like a customer while building out a project, but it is something you should always keep in mind. Have you ever visited a site with a lot of really cool Flash features, but you couldn't figure out how to navigate to anything? Or have you been bored waiting for a site to load? Ever visited a site that opens a popup after every link you click on? Or have you not been able to read anything on the site because the font size was too small or the text and background colors were too dramatic?

Too often, as web designers, we make the mistake of building something that we can finish quickly, forgetting to plan for the future. This is a very dangerous prospect if you haven't taken the customer into consideration. If you forget to serve the end user you will waste time and money starting over. Occasionally, there may be a feature or function of your site that must be implemented where it doesn't provide the best customer interaction; this should be the exception and not the rule.

All About the Customer means that each part of the landing page exists to either further the customer through the buying/lead generation process, or to explain a feature of the site that a customer may have a question about. Nothing on the site detracts from the buying process, and nothing on the site should cause the customer to become confused to the point where it feels like he or she should submit negative feedback.

So, why would you change your website to All About the Customer? If your site exit surveys or customer feedback indicate moderately to highly unsatisfied customer interaction; your landing page has a large amount of clicks on your customer service links (not the Your Account links); visitors have a high time on-page combined with a high single page visit rate; you have a high amount of page views per visit; and/or if your visitors simply aren't interacting with your landing page as you expected they would, then this chapter will give you a unique idea for redesign.

Site exit surveys along with customer submitted feedback will typically tell you what customers like and don't like about your website. We highly recommend that if you are not using site exit survey, and/or a customer feedback tool that you add these tools immediately. Your feedback tool should remain consistent on your site, while your site exit surveys can be deployed on a monthly or quarterly basis. Please keep in mind that often this kind of reporting can be skewed toward the vocal customers—not the majority. Also customers with negative experiences are more apt to leave feedback as opposed to those who have a positive experience.

In this chapter we discuss the positives and negatives of Travelocity™'s service in the summer and fall of 2008 in relation to how it could be an All About the Customer website. In addition, we discuss elements that should be tested to determine whether they can be eliminated, edited, or enhanced depending on whether or not they are necessary to further the customer in the buying process. Again, we touch on key analytics that you can use to measure whether the changes made have helped improve your landing page. Finally, we close with next steps that are determined by what your analysis shows.

Site Design

What about your site design can affect how a potential new user interacts with your site and brand? Here are some positives and negatives we have seen in the travel industry.

Positives:

- **Account Login is in the upper right corner**—it is cliché to say, but the upper right hand corner is prime territory in your design. If you want to make a website feel more focused on the customer, this is a good place to put something that is valuable to them.

- **Have a branded credit card with travel rewards**—a branded rewards system makes an immediate statement that you value your visitors' business. It can also communicate a greater level of investment in their satisfaction.

- **Have a prominent, well-publicized guarantee**—guarantees and customer protection are keystones in a human approach to business. This is a very important element to highlight.

- **Have a fare tracker**—the fare tracker allows users to put interaction on their terms. For research-minded and relationship-minded users this is a communication that you value their process.

- **Greeting when you are logged in**—a simple reward for logged in users. Greet them. But, don't take this as an endpoint. Personalization means much more than displaying their name.

- **Secondary resources**—Travelocity™ has taken their primary function—travel—and coupled it with a secondary human response to travel—sharing pictures. What is a secondary function that you can offer to support your main purpose?

- **Windows Vista Widget**—widgets allow interaction to happen in a much lower attention way, giving the power back to the user.

- **Travel alerts**—this is a recent addition to many travel sites, however this is a very nice customer-oriented feature. It also gives somewhat of a human feel to the website. It links to notices such as current hurricane information and extra baggage pricing. Relationship-driven users find this type of extra support to be very valuable.

- **Site search**—if you have a large site with lots of content, you should be offering a direct solution for finding information. On smaller sites this can be accomplished with a well-structured annotated sitemap.

Negatives:

- **Redundant Account Links**—redundancy is confusing in web content. Usability best practices tell us that customers need a clear path to follow; having multiple links to the same area causes customer confusion. Example: if you have links for both Login and Account, which one lets you see your flight itinerary? Note that this does not mean that more than one route to the same section is bad, but you should avoid using synonyms. My Flights and Account may be the same place—even though they communicate different immediate needs.

- **Redundant links in general**—if you are going to have a link in the main content that can be found elsewhere, make it one or two links that you are trying to feature. Do not duplicate all or most links as this does not allow for a clear path for the customer to follow.

- **Too much going on**—many sites fall into a trap of putting all of their information on the page all the time. This makes the site feel piecemeal and cluttered. Many users, especially new users, will become frustrated by not being able to figure out where to find what they want.

- **Logo inconsistent with branding**—again, use Travelocity™ as an example. While commercials typically end with a screen that shows the logo seen on the website, the Travelocity™ gnome is by far the most recognizable part of the commercial. The gnome can be found on the site but is not part of their logo.[1] We recommend making a connection between your logo and other brand images. In this case Travelocity™ could create a "Find the Gnome" game on their website to encourage visitors to interact more with the website (this may be a better fit for All About Lasting Relationships)

- **Dropped user sessions**—technical difficulties are a given with technology, but as of December 2008 Firefox® is the second most popular browser, after Microsoft ® Internet Explorer.[2] Depending on your particular business you may be losing trust from 12–20 percent of your potential business because of a broken process. Make sure that your programming does not limit users to only one technology.

- **No telephone contact information on home page**—high customer service means freeing visitors form their computers. Do not forsake offline strengths/opportunities when designing your website.

- **Confusing function unit**—avoid link redundancy between the function unit and the top navigation, and possibly even other main content. To continue the travel example: default to the broadest option. Let the customer choose a time if they want, but don't make them choose Anytime and certainly make sure that the Anytime option is available to them. Customers are much smarter these days

---

[1] While the gnome example is a good example of branding inconsistency, we are not affiliated with Travelociy and as such do not know whether there is a legal ramification of using the gnome in their logo.

[2] http://www.w3schools.com/browsers/browsers_stats.asp

and they know that they may find a better deal if they search through all time slots. Finally, Submit buttons need to be located near the last option the visitor interacts with. If your user needs to search for the Submit button you are losing trust.

To make your site customer-centric you probably need to make some design overhauls. Examples include, but are not limited to: putting the lightest background behind the customer interaction points (dark background with white text is generally a bad customer experience); removing the redundant account link (these cause confusion); increasing the size of the greeting when logged in (it doesn't do any good if they don't see it); putting the guarantee in a more prominent placement; putting the reward system (e.g. credit card) in a more prominent placement; and making customer care more visible (you can't be customer-centric if you don't put their needs first). You also need to minimize any situations where a user would have to sign in more than once.

Off-site Issues

- **Frequent customer service complaints**—win the war on your squeaky wheels by openly addressing their issues. Make it impossible for anyone to not resolve a similar issue in a timely fashion.

- **Follow your guarantee**—don't publicize a guarantee unless you are going to make good every time.

- **Call center complaints**—this one is big. Poor support means that you have failed to fulfill the promise of your brand. Paradoxically, previous failures can offer a clear path to expanding and solidifying a brand of customer service. However, this means investing in retroactive problem solving.

- **Have a public figure**—Dan@Sprint.com has been a powerful ad campaign for Sprint, in that it has generated buzz on the internet and at dinner conversations. If you are a small to medium business you have a distinct advantage; your "Dan" can be the real person behind the email. It is of particular importance that any public figure be well supported, as they will become a lightning rod for all complaints from that point forward.

Crossing into the upper echelon of service means taking the culture off-site. This means not making people wait on hold too long. One common complaint about many major brands is that you may spend from 45 to 120 minutes on a call that ends in unresolved billing issues. If you can't get through to customer service they can't help you. Don't tell your customers their time is important **unless you are offering a solution to their problem immediately** (e.g. "We respect your time. Email callme@website.com with your name and phone number and a representative will call you").

Every company needs to be more open about their refund policy and specify times in real terms (days/weeks), not business days. To be "The Best Guarantee On The Web" means having the shortest payback wait period at the minimum. Having the best customer service also means having short wait times and high standards for the language skills of phone operators. Many complaints these days are the result of outsourced call centers and sound like this: "No resolution and difficult, hard to understand call center." Fixing the above problems will result in a much higher satisfaction rate.

BizRate® gave all the top travel sites 87 percent satisfaction from June to October of 2008; if anyone could hit 95 percent they could make a great branding move of it. The same is likely true in your industry.

According to JD Power's assessment of online travel, Travelocity™ loses to Hotwire™ for highest satisfaction on only one metric—overall satisfaction. Travelocity™ wins five stars for ease of booking, appearance, and navigation, and four stars overall. The complaints all center on offline interactions and advertising truthfulness. If your business has an advertisement for anything it should be echoed immediately on your site, and fulfilled with gusto.

Things That Will Tip the Scales

- **Offer defaulting to account page for logged in users**—this is one of the quiet rewards you can offer a loyal customer. This is your opportunity to do real customization—to transcend one of the common failings of the Internet in the eye of relationship-driven customers. Greetings are the first step toward customization, but they are commonplace. Allowing a customer to log in and see a customized account page for the duration of their session gives them a high level of interaction without much extra effort on your part. Let them have it their way.

- **Include the function unit in "My Stuff"**—the account sections of most sites do not allow the visitor to fulfill the primary function of the site from their account page. Forcing customers to choose between account and function is a multiplying loss.

- **Offer a protection on your guarantee**—what happens when you fail to deliver on your guarantee? Put this information in your guarantee: *If we can't solve your problem in five days we will _____ .* This is part of creating a culture of responsibility that supports genuine customer care.

- **Implement widgets for all the major services, not just Microsoft®**—this is similar to dropping sessions in Firefox®. If you drop the customer care with a significant portion of your customers you will have growing trouble fulfilling a brand of customer care. The most common issue is only making widgets for Microsoft users. We suggest that you look into additional support including Google™ Gadgets, Pageflakes, OSX Dashboard, and iPhone™ applications.

- **Implement SMS for delays/notification**—in the case of travel there are unstoppable and unforeseeable problems that can occur. A small effort for you can be turned into a major time saver for your user. Think along the lines of your major service (e.g. if you have a ski resort alert expected arrivals via text message if the pass closes).

- **Implement response for fare tracker**—all of the major travel aggregates have an RSS feed that will let you get ongoing updates on flights/vacations you want. But they have not implemented a feedback system. When your offering loses value it becomes a piece of background noise. By implementing a simple "I like this trip" option it can become genuinely personalized, more like Pandora® (an Internet radio station that lets you give yes/no feedback on the songs they play for you).

- **Offer rewards for repeat use (outside of the credit card offer)**—the credit card is a standard for the travel industry, the way a member card is with groceries, but it has limited appeal. If the customer doesn't want another card it is a barrier to integrating loyalty rewards. Expedia® uses a system that puts you in the rewards system and gives you a bonus on the credit card.

Communication

Designing a site that is heavily focused on customer acquisition means taking extra steps to solidify customer communication. There are several organizations that regularly engage in customer feedback and testimonials: BizRate®, AngiesList, MedFinds.com, BarFly.com, etc. In every industry there is an organization that collects reviews online. Making your website and services accessible to relationship-driven people means integrating your brand into these portals. If you have made the decision that you are going to focus on humanistic users, you should be leveraging other organizations that service this type of customer.

Usability Testing

We highly recommend that you conduct usability tests in conjunction with each change that you make. You should develop one or more prototypes and then test each against the others with customers. This should be done well before you go live with any change online. You may have to go through several iterations before you have changes that you are comfortable with based on customer test reaction.

Things that should be tested:

- Placement of Guarantee—while we still want to preach that the function unit should be the main point of emphasis on your site, you should test the placement of your guarantee. With Travelocity™, they should reduce the number of Sale/Discount banners in their content area and move the guarantee to a prominent location to see if it gets clicks and/or if feedback complaints go down. In addition, we recommend a popover (popovers are not really a window but rather just another layer on the page itself) for the guarantee so that the visitor is not leaving the buying funnel, but simply gathering more information to make a better decision. (See glossary for full popover definition.)

- Branded Credit card—there are two options with the credit card. Option one: make the link to the credit card a popover that gives the customer more information with another link they can click to sign up for the credit card. This keeps the visitor from fully leaving the buying process and if they decide against the credit card they can simply click a close button and they'll still be on the landing page and won't have to navigate back to the process. If they do decide to apply, once they have done so there should be a prominent link back to the function unit page. Option two: Keep the credit card located as is, but make it a prominent feature of the "My Stuff" page. With this option if the customer decides to apply there should be a prominent link to the function unit once the application is finalized.

- Use of login—where do visitors log in on your site? Is the current strategy effective without taking away from the function unit?

- Use of alternate home—A/B testing on your landing/home page can be done for any of the suggested changes, however here we are specifically talking about using an alternate home page if your visitor is logged in.

- Response rate to reward offers—in most industries, if you offer a reward, you'll see a spike in traffic and sales, however there's typically a unique ROI that you must find: where is that perfect point?

- Download of widget—typically the link that a visitor clicks on from an RSS or from a widget will have a code appended that will tell your analytics program where the visitor came from to get to your site; however, tracking the number of widget downloads will tell you whether this feature remains effective at getting new visitors to sign up for a feed. This will be explored further in "All About Retention."

Analysis

The overarching goal of the All About the Customer concept is retaining a good click-through rate to your function unit, reducing errors on your site, and reducing the number of customer complaints about your site. By slightly reducing the number of choices and focusing on some of your customer-oriented features you are catering to customer-focused mindsets and those visitors who believe that great customer service is priceless. Unless your customers feel your site is terrible, focusing more on the customer will not bring drastic change to most of your top line metrics, but you should see your customer service rating go up.

Any time you make a change that benefits the customer you will see some positive shifts in your data. The main metrics you should use to measure the effectiveness of this change are site exit surveys and customer feedback forums, time spent on landing page/bounce rate, top clicks report for landing page/home page, page views per visit, visitor to buyer path completion, function unit submits, and site conversion.

Disclaimer

Please keep in mind that any major changes, even positive ones, will scare some users. It is important to pair these results with other metrics and not evaluate success or failure by just one metric.

Voice of Customer: Exit Surveys and Customer Feedback Forums

Exit surveys can tell you why a customer left your website without purchasing. Typically, the customer will answer a multiple choice question or they will give a one to five rating. Feedback is typically open forum and you will get plenty of interesting and useful comments. Typically the service that you use will have a tool that can filter by department or keyword. Finally, you have third-party services such as BizRate®, who conduct anonymous studies of individuals and compile data that will rank your site based on certain criteria. You can use all three of these forums to gauge whether your changes have a positive impact on what the customer thinks about your site in general as well as about a particular section or feature of your site. Obviously if the ratings go down or you get an increased amount of negative feedback then you still have some work to do and should consider some of our other suggestions for changes.

Time On-page Versus Bounce Rate

An increase in time on-page by itself would suggest that visitors are confused about what to do on your site. However, if bounce rate goes up as well, this would confirm that either your navigation, layout, or site intent are not intuitive and need to be improved. Also, you could combine time on-page with page views per visit and if these are both increased, customers are probably confused by your site or they are not finding what they are looking for.

Click-Through Rate for Links on Landing Page

If you see an increasing amount of clicks on your customer service links or to your site map, your site might need some work. Keep in mind that while these links may not be top-clicked links overall, if they see a dramatic increase, it means that customers are probably confused.

A common cause of searching is not remembering where goal information is or what it is called in the system. Make sure you have names that make sense for your features.

If you have numerous sections of your landing page that get no clicks you should be considering what information will make an actual difference in its place. Looking to what your site map is actually used for or high traffic pages outside your conversion funnel is a good place to start when making a featured links block.

Pages per Visit and Page Views

While the bottom line is booking, this focuses on the customer as well. Successful changes should move your pages per visit slightly above the number of pages required to complete a transaction, since you expect them to read at least one of the customer service areas before making a decision.

If you have a high amount of page views per visit you should be focusing on prominent customer service areas, bringing them structurally closer to your transaction funnel. However, if this number inflates dramatically, you should consider another architecture change—one that reduces the need to leave the path to completion. Again, you want to see this number just slightly above the actual number of pages it takes to get from landing page to checkout. You'll want users to click on the guarantee and/or the credit card link, read the info, and then get back into the buying process.

If you decide to make the guarantee and/or credit card a popover, you'll probably use Flash or Ajax to do this. Because these are not actual pages, you'll have to use some specialty tagging to record that the visitor viewed this page. Typically this special tag can be counted as a page view. The popover option will keep your page views per visitor to a relatively close number to what you want it to be, as there will be less navigation involved for the customer to get back to the function unit. However, you will want to pay special attention to these pages, as any page outside your completion path that sees a noticeable increase is a possible bottleneck to your completion.

Visitor to Buyer Path Completion

If you currently track visitor to buyer path completion then you'll want to see that the ratios on each step increase. If they do, your goal of making your site more customer-friendly has been reached. If they do not, then you need to consider some of the other changes suggested in this book.

Here's an example of what your data might look like:

If you have 1,000 visitors, and only 500 make it to a product/browse page, you have to ask yourself where else 50 percent of your initial visitors are moving. Also, if after redesign, you see this number increase then obviously your landing page is working better at driving visitors to the buying process. If this number drops, first check to see if overall conversion has dropped as well. If it has then you can also check page abandonment and time on-site. If abandonment is up and time on-site is down then it is safe to say that this option for a landing page is not appealing to your customer. If abandonment is up and time on-site is also up, it could either mean that visitors are not sure of what to do next, or are possibly getting side tracked with something on a particular page. If abandonment is the same or down but time on-site is up, it could mean that something about the page is distracting the visitor and keeping them from moving forward in the process, so further changes may need to be made. Alternately this could mean that you are attracting more Researcher customers that are actually reading more of your content. You need to separate out which issue you have by running some tests to see how closely your time on-page resembles the time it takes to read all of the content. Grab a couple of people and ask them to read the entire page while you time them.

Finally, let's say prior to redesign 1,000 visitors came to your landing page and 600 went on to a browse page, 200 added to cart, and 25 made a purchase; after redesign 1,000 visitors came to your landing page, 700 went on to a browse page, 200 added to card, and 25 made a purchase. If you only looked at conversion, you wouldn't see a positive change in overall conversion, so you would possibly be disappointed and might make the mistake of deciding that your landing page changes aren't working; you might revert back. The pathing report actually shows you that your landing page was more successful at driving visitors forward in the process; however, cart completion in this example is the same. What this means is that you need to look at the rest of the shopping process. However, that is not going to be addressed in this text. It could possibly mean your conversion is maxed at 2.5 percent, or maybe it's just not the right season for you. Possibly, you may need to review your product set to see if you are offering a competitive product.

Function Unit Submits

This will give you a different number than page conversion. With this you can divide the total number of submits by the total number of unique visits (sessions) to find out if making the guarantee and/or offering a credit card along with some navigation changes leads to more submits. If it does, then obviously you have achieved your main goal (and this should be your main goal). If this number goes down, you should verify whether page abandonment has gone up along with time on-page. Also check your page conversion and site conversion. If conversion is down, submits are down, and abandonment is up you can determine that this method is not right for your landing page.

If you don't already track submit to unique visit rate, you can find this data by either adding a click event tag on the Submit button, or with certain services that use specialty tags like a form tag, event tag, or element tag. This will probably give you a number specific to how many unique submits versus unique visits your page produces. If you are receiving submits in a number that suggests multiple submits per user you need to establish why. Possible process issues that cause multiple submits include technical problems and browser users. If you are getting many requests from your visitors it means that you are either not fulfilling their needs on some level or you have an opportunity to capitalize on a buying behavior.

High submit to total conversions should be a point of great attention. If you are attracting browsing/researching visitors it is important to consider very specific measures to increase that particular group's satisfaction and consider retention-based changes. Researchers tend not to be at a decision point; you need to either help them to that point or solidify loyalty before they reach the point of action.

If your users aren't displaying research behavior then high submit to conversion is a red flag for a broken transaction process. In e-commerce terms the problem indicator would be cart abandonment. If the changes you are making have put users in your sales funnel but they aren't closing then you have a clear indicator that something in your funnel may be the barrier to conversion.

Site Conversion

Site conversion is a widely used performance indicator because this metric gives you the bare bones measurement of whether your site is successful at generating a lead or getting an order (or whatever else is the intent of your site). Conversion rate as a metric is typically used as the safety net for other metrics. While site conversion is a great bar to evaluate your site, it doesn't ever tell the entire story, and thus other metrics should be used in conjunction with it.

Understanding why people convert is more important than the number of completions. Looking into the supporting parts, like clickpath and exits, will tell you more about why you are making conversions than the conversion rate will tell you.

Now What?

If your business already has an offline component you want to accentuate the qualities that make your business successful offline and bring them to your online presence. For many local businesses value proposition revolves around more human aspects. So, we have chosen Travelocity™ as an example of a more human approach to web business; a concept that we call All About The Customer.

For the web marketers reading this book, have you ever clicked on a natural listing and found the subject of your search three or more pages deep into the site and not actually part of the landing page? Or worse, you clicked on a paid link for a term and the subject is nowhere to be found on the landing page? These are typically much easier mistakes to fix than a poorly functioning website.

However, with today's technology and web use, if you have a website with a terrible customer experience your visitors will talk about it to anyone who will listen. If a visitor searches Google™ for you and couldn't find what they were looking for after clicking on your link, they are sure to let anyone and everyone know about it. Granted, there are times when a less customer friendly option to your site may win out over the customer preferred option, but as a general rule, whether or not your customer understands your functionality should always be the deciding factor in how you build your site.

In the All About The Customer scenario you should be specifically clued in on the use and engagement of additive features, like widgets and alternative home pages—they will be an important indicator of the type of customers you are bringing in. Of the scenarios we have put together this one is probably most aided by customer feedback before changes. Ask a few of your repeat customers what features they would be interested in seeing.

All About Retention

"Do what you do so well that they will want to see it again and bring their friends."

- Walt Disney

Why do visitors come to your website? More importantly, why do they choose your website as their *favorite*—as opposed to a competitor's website? Do the changes you make to your site increase or decrease your customer loyalty? As marketers and web developers you must be able to answer these questions before you make a change to your site. If you do not, you will get inconsistent results.

A great way to answer the above questions is to turn the tables on website interaction. What websites do you enjoy visiting and what website do you have in your favorites? If website XYZ took away feature A, would you still enjoy your visit? Typically you can get away with small tweaks to your website without much consequence, but major changes should have major implications. Your repeat visitors create a foundation for your business, typically convert higher, and typically visit more often than new visitors. They know your website and recognize changes. Your best customers are most likely to leave you unsolicited feedback about your site, saving you time and effort.

There are many measurable channels that lead a visitor to a website, such as paid and natural search, related site links, and media ads. Everything else is lumped together into what is commonly called direct navigation or direct load—television and radio ads that incorporate an easy to remember web address, print or billboard ads that can be typed in to your browser, word of mouth referrals that lead to a visitor typing in your domain name directly. However, this set of visitors actually only makes up a small portion of your total direct navigation since more often than not your repeat and loyal customers will direct load into your home page/landing page. Finally, the problem with all of the above options is that every other site has just about as many portals leading a visitor to their website.

The difference between a good website and one that needs improvement is the amount of repeat visitors it has. It is your job to figure out how to differentiate your website enough that a visitor will want to return to it multiple times. Repeat visitors are typically your loyal customers, and either have your home page/landing page saved as a favorite or they know your web address by heart and make up the largest portion of your direct navigation numbers.

Why Should I Care About This?

Repeat visitors typically convert better than new visitors and the reason is simple: trust and loyalty. What leads customers to feel trust in and loyalty to a site? Ease of use, strong branding, good customer service, and dependable products. If you have most of these things, chances are you have a good repeat visitor base. If you do not, these are things you need to improve upon.

It's important to remember that retention also means growing your existing customer base. So while you should focus on ensuring that the changes you make do not negatively affect your existing customer, you should study your data to see if your new customer conversion could be increased by any changes that would not adversely affect the existing customer. Also, your search links, web media, affiliate, and referral marketing should focus on getting new qualified visitors to the site while at the same time not discouraging your existing customers from entering the site via one of these channels.

The following approach assumes that you have a solid website already: good functionality, speedy page load, basic website essentials like site search, telephone contact information, distinct and user friendly function unit, and clear buying path. If you have all of the above, you should have a strong conversion rate and strong sales. However, if this is not the case and sales or conversion are not on par with your competition, or maybe just not where you'd like them to be, this chapter will help you figure out what else you can do.

In this chapter we discuss the positives and negatives of an All About Retention website. We discuss elements that should be tested to determine whether they can be eliminated, edited, or enhanced depending on whether they are necessary to further the customer in the buying process. Further, we touch on key analytics that you can use to measure whether the changes made have helped improve your landing page. Finally, we close with next steps that are determined by what your analysis shows.

Site Design

What if you already have strong traffic for your industry? You are well positioned to transition to the All About Retention model. Here are some changes to keep in mind.

Positives:

- **Account Login is in the upper right corner**—it is cliché to say, and we have said it several times, but the upper right hand corner is prime territory in your design. If you want to make a website feel more focused on the customer this is a good place to put something that is valuable to them.

- **Branding of their "mascot" with their logo**—unlike Travelocity™, Expedia®'s mascot is not as well known, but their yellow suitcase with an airplane circling a globe can be seen at the end of their commercials and in their web ads. They have incorporated the airplane and globe into their site logo which ties the mascot to the logo fairly well.

- **Make use of top navigation**—of the major travel sites, Expedia is the only one that uses "Rewards" as a category. Keep your top navigation useful and avoid redundancy. Consider how you can make your offering just a little easier than your competition's.

- **Make the main content clean**—separate your messages. Keep the main function and the secondary offerings clearly delineated so users don't question what they are doing. Some sites use columns to keep a visual division of their offerings like up sell and long sale elements.

- **Use empowerment messaging**—brand with second person language, like "Build Your Trip," and then include distinct mascots for each section of the function unit. This gives the visitor a sense that this site is more than just a one-time shop, but rather a place to visit frequently for an enjoyable experience. Options like "Your

Itineraries" and "Find Your Perfect Trip" give the visitor a sense that they have a customized place to come to research and book their travel needs.

- **Telephone contact information prominent**—ensure that the customer knows what number to call with questions, comments, concerns, or if he or she feels the need to book with a live person. This is a very important addition for serving relationship-driven users.

- **Uncouple your reward system**—a branded rewards system makes an immediate statement that you value your customers' business. It can also communicate a greater level of investment in their satisfaction. Create a reward system that does not require a high level of user investment.

- **Have a prominent, well-publicized guarantee**—guarantees and customer protection are keystones in a human approach to business. This is a very important element to highlight.

- **Have an RSS feed**—low investment updates allow users to put interaction on their terms. For research-minded and relationship-minded users this is a communication that you value their process.

- **Greeting when you are logged in**—a simple reward for logged in users. Greet them. But, don't take this as an endpoint personalization means much more than displaying their name.

- **Site search**—if you have a large site with lots of content you should be offering a direct solution for finding information. If you have a larger site with multiple category pages, having the on-site search box gives the visitor comfort that if they can't find something they can just search for it. Typically retail websites see anywhere from 15-40 percent of their traffic using on-site search so this feature is a must have.

- **Mobile Web**—according to a *Shaping the Future of the Newspaper* article, mobile web users in the U.S. totaled 37 million in 2007 and are expected to grow at 19 percent per year thru 2012—putting the number at 92 million or roughly 30 percent of the U.S. population. Much more, sales from mobile web are expected to by 1.4 billion dollars by 2012.[1]

- **Alerts**—you should offer alerts in more than one way. RSS, email, and text messages about new opportunities have all become valid options for continued communication.

- **Localization**—many sites utilize cookie information to make special offers to you such as cheap flights from your local airport and travel deals to various locations from your local airport.

- **Extensive logged in benefits**—one of the features that Expedia® offers that is particularly valuable to relationship-driven users is a travel arranger that allows one user to permit another user to schedule a trip for them. Reducing barriers in user-to-user interaction is a revolution in many industries where the idea of community is still in its infancy.

Negatives:

---

[1] http://www.sfnblog.com/index.php/2008/09/19/2316-mobile-web-users-search-revenue-grow-in-us

- **Paid search links take you to a generic landing page**—if you are paying per click, you should ensure that your customer is directed to a landing page that is customized to the term. For example, if you want to differentiate your brand for customer support you need to incorporate consistent messages in your advertising that are echoed on your site, leaving a clear trail and repeated indication that the visitor is making progress.

- **Main content has mixed messages**—your main function should be clearly marked. While it is important to show off the thing your service has that your competitors don't, you shouldn't let that detract from your main purpose.

- **Random banner advertisement at bottom of the page**—are you showing an advertisement at the bottom of your page? Get rid of this advertisement; if the visitor makes it to the bottom of the page they need something more than another advertisement to solve their problem. Unless you are handsomely monetized through advertising, you have something more important to do with your space than advertise.

- **Too much page below the fold**—as your site grows your content should become more specific from page to page. If you are making people scroll on most pages you probably have an opportunity to streamline.

- **Too much content in the "Deals" section**—if it has a whole category to itself you don't need to dedicate more than a third of your design to advertising it.

To make your site retention-centric you need to make some design overhauls including, but not limited to, reducing the amount of content area dedicated to deals and sales, refocusing that area on continued relationship links, and adding RSS feeds, brand-exclusive links, rewards links, and a guarantee.

Offline Issues

Expedia® offers a price guarantee on their flights. This guarantee had been called the best in the industry until the spring of 2008 when Orbitz™ matched this price guarantee. With most guarantees there are a lot of loopholes that favor the company and not the customer. Expedia could separate itself from the pack by amending its price guarantee to favor a customer if the price booked is not the lowest price. Having a simple guarantee is clear brand opportunity. The potential for word of mouth and trust around a clear understandable price protection can be huge.

You should always try to address any complaints and ensure that your customer service is high in quality. Even if you have a good customer image right now, you want to continue to avoid complaints. Customer retention and loyalty can be greatly served by implementing proactive rather than reactive customer service. Find a common issue, have your customer service department preempt a few people that may have experience, and elicit feedback to improve your positive reviews.

Communication

Creating a site that is heavily focused on customer retention means taking extra steps to solidify customer communication. Regular emails to your premium customers for incentives and special sales can help drive conversion and sales for your site. Keeping your best customers informed of coming changes also gives them a feeling of community, special treatment, and gives them another reason to come back to your site knowing that they were one of the first few to see the changes. Order confirmation emails that arrive with a personal touch such as a customer's first name in the "Dear" section, shopping cart expiration emails, and sale reminder emails are all effective ways of communicating and converting your existing customer base.

If you have the ability to tie an email address to a visitor who has visited several times but never purchased, an email for 10 percent off their first purchase might help get the conversion and solidify that visitor as growth to your existing customer base. Other proactive customer service communications include offering an email discount to repeat users who haven't booked in a while, calling to assist users who have experienced an involuntary cancellation, or contacting frequent users to thank them for their business.

Usability Testing

We highly recommend that you conduct usability tests with each change you make. You should develop one or more prototypes and then test each against the other with customers. This should be done well before you go live with any change online. You may have to go through several iterations before you have changes that you are comfortable with based on customer test reaction.

Things that should be tested:

- Main content versus sale/discount content—many websites devote too much space to sales and discount content. Try giving more attention to your main purpose to make the specials more special.

- Rewards—if you are using a reward/thank you system you should consider visually connecting it to offers that are exclusive to your service.

- Use of login—where do visitors log in on your site? Is the current link strategy effective without taking away from the function unit?

- Use of alternate home—A/B testing on your landing/home page can be done for any of the suggested changes, however here we are specifically talking about using an alternate home page if your visitor is logged in. Test which category landing pages are most effective for landing paid search customers.

- Downloads—try advertising your takeaways in different ways. If you are using a widget or PDF that has live links you should append special tracking to them to ensure they are easily differentiated in your web analytics program.

- Background color versus text color—even though we generally recommend light background and dark text that does not mean that the only option is black and white.

Analysis

The overarching goal of the All About Retention concept is to retain a good click rate to your function unit, ensuring that your customer service and account links are distinct, and slightly turning the focus of the site towards the tools and amenities that separate your site from your competition. By slightly reducing the number of choices and focusing on some of your extra features, you are catering to the repeat visitor and to the loyal visitor while enticing new customers with features not seen on competitors' sites.

Again, this section assumes that your conversion and sales are meeting your expectations and you are interested in what more you can do to improve your site and your numbers. Thus, whole conversion is not considered a key metric for this chapter; however, you should verify that conversion does not decrease any time you make a change to your site. Key metrics to verify All About Retention changes include new versus return visitors, new versus return buyers, new versus return visitor conversion, segmentation reports, page views per session, time spent on-site, click path analysis, landing page click analysis, and click path reporting. Qualitative reporting such as customer satisfaction rating and customer feedback reports should also be reviewed to ensure that visitors are enjoying their experience.

Disclaimer

Please keep in mind that any major changes, even positive ones, will scare some users. It is important to pair these results with other metrics and not evaluate success or failure by just one metric.

Segmentation Analysis

Segmentation analysis allows you to view your data for a specific group of people; in this case you want to segment by new versus return visitors and starts from account versus starts from home page. This will give you insight into your interaction and engagement metrics on your site and within your subcategories.

New vs. Return Visitors

You should be separating the amount of new versus return visitors out of your total unique visitor numbers. While you want to see the percentage breakout between these change (a drop in new visitor volume could mean you are not marketing enough to your new visitor channels), you do want to see your return visitor number continue to climb over time. Also, repeat visitors (visitors who visit your site more than once during a measured timeframe) should be steady or increasing. If either your return or repeat visitor numbers drop, these visitors do not like your changes and have stopped coming to the site altogether and you need to check your customer feedback forum for more information. Considering these are your more loyal customers, it is a major indicator that your changes were not positive if they stop coming to the site altogether.

New vs. Return Buyers

New buyers are not necessarily new to the site; however, if you can determine that a particular group of visitors are return visitors (meaning they have previously visited the site) and they become new buyers (meaning they have never purchased on your site before), you can positively attribute your landing page changes to that sale. On the other hand if you see a drop in return buyers, it could indicate that the changes you've made have had a negative impact on your most loyal customers (those who have previously made a purchase on your site). This would be a good indicator that you need to either revert back or make an additional change.

New vs. Return Conversion

You want to see both new and return conversions increase. If you continue to hold a steady amount of return/repeat visitors, but conversions start to drop, it could mean that either your product set is stale and needs to be refreshed, your action path is broken, or there are some changes that are negatively affecting your repeat visitors' viewing habits. If they are still visiting the site they probably haven't left any negative feedback, they are just unsure how to complete their order since they were used to doing it differently before the site change. Keep in mind that a return/repeat conversion drop could also mean that your return and repeat visitors are *shoppers* but not *buyers*. They use the website to find products they like and then visit a retail location and buy it. If repeat conversions increase, you have done your job properly and this was the correct change for you to make (for now).

Pages per Visit and Page/Element Views

While the bottom line in this scenario is completed conversions, retention is more about how engaged with the site the visitor is. Successful changes should move your pages per visit slightly above the number of pages required to complete a transaction, since you want them to read at least one of the added benefit areas before making a decision. You should not have had a high number of page views per visit prior to redesign and while this number should increase a bit, you do not want the increase to be too dramatic as this takes away from making a buying decision. If this number inflates dramatically, then you should consider a different design change. Again, you want to see this number slightly above the actual number of pages it takes to get from landing page to checkout. You'll want them to click on the rewards programs and the email sign up links and read the info and then get back into the buying process.

With most browsers today enabling a popup blocker, you may decide to make the rewards points a popover. You will probably use DHTML, Ajax, or

Flash to do this. Because these are not actual pages, you may have to use some specialty tagging to record that the visitor viewed this page. Typically this special tag can be counted as a page view if you so choose. The popover option will keep your page views per visitor to a number relatively close to what you want it to be, as there will be less navigation involved for the customer to get back to the function unit. However, you will want to pay special attention to these pages as any page that is outside your completion path that sees a noticeable increase is a possible bottleneck to your completion.

Similar to the All About Speed scenario, you may want to consider creating a sub-domain to handle certain categories. Creating a profile that specifically segments your Account Section as an entrance to the action path will help you understand how your return users interact with the repeat buying process.

Time Spent On-site

An increase in time on-page by itself would suggest that visitors are more engaged on your site. However, if this number goes up too much, it could mean that you've confused your customer. You can pair time on-page with page views per visit and if these are both increased then visitors are engaged in your site and as long as conversion remains on par or increases then this is a win for your redesign.

Visitor to Conversion Path Completion

If you currently track visitor to conversion path completion then you'll want to see that the ratios on each step increase. If they do, your goal of making your site more customer friendly has been reached. If they do not, then you need to consider some of the other changes suggested in this book.

The pathing scenario described in All About the Customer could apply here as well.

Top Clicks Report for Landing Page

If you see a large amount of clicks on your customer service links or to your site map, your site might need some work. Keep in mind that while these links may not be top-clicked links overall, if they see a dramatic increase it means that customers are looking for something. You do want to see increases to your additional tools links, however, without seeing a huge negative impact to the function unit clicks.

Click Path Reporting

Click path reporting will break out the top-clicked path step-by-step from landing page to order completion. This gives you more of a three dimensional view of how visitors are interacting with your site as a whole. Look particularly for top exit pages and top time on-page. These two places are keystones to streamlining your conversion process. Specifically a click path that starts from your home page and ends at the top exit page is problematic. In the scenario of All About Retention you have an opportunity to implement proactive customer service by contacting a few logged in users and asking why they left that particular section of your site. Invite them to tell you how you can better serve them and reap the rewards of their sense of value.

Function Unit Submits

Like conversion, this is not a key metric for this type of redesign, however it is still important to measure. If this number goes down, you should segment the page to see how repeat visitors' interaction has changed. If the numbers still look bad then you should consider making another revision. While you want to increase traffic to the other portions of your site, you do not want to take away from the function unit, as this is still the main point of your site.

If your retention efforts were successful you will want to see at least a stable percentage of return user conversions, but even a drop here is a win if you see expanded use of account functions and retention elements, such as rewards and subscriptions.

Voice of the Customer: Exit Surveys and Customer Feedback Forums

As stated in the previous chapter, exit surveys can tell you why a customer left your website without purchasing. You can use any of the three forums (questionnaire/ratings, free form, live chat) to gauge whether your changes have a positive impact on what the customer thinks of your site in general or a particular section or feature of it. Obviously if the ratings go downward or if you get an increased amount of negative feedback you still have some work to do and should consider some of our other suggestions for changes. In many cases customers who leave feedback are upset by something so your feedback may not be very positive. Keep in mind that negative feedback can sometimes be more helpful than positive feedback. There is always a reason why someone does not make a purchase on your website and it is probably more beneficial for you to know why he or she did NOT buy versus simply knowing that a purchase was made.

As for long-term retention feedback, being able to lure back customers who did not buy will certainly help long-term retention. Knowing the new challenges that your website faces will allow you to keep your website fresh and competitive. Sometimes our best customers end up being our best critics because they become accustomed to being pleased every time they enter the website. When something doesn't go right for them they are quick to tell us about it. Finally, knowing your shortcomings will allow you to control the negative buzz around your website. As you can see, the Jeff Bezos quote from "All About the Customer" is applicable to this chapter as well.

Now What?

If your site already had good conversion and sales, and you have determined that this change has made a positive impact, then it's time to sit back, relax, and reap the rewards. Ok, not seriously, but you can breathe a little easier. At this point you probably should follow the "if it ain't broke then don't fix it" methodology. Continue to monitor customer feedback forums to ensure that visitors to your site have a good experience. Continue to monitor your key metrics and feel free to expand on the recommended metrics. Specifically, you should utilize a customer engagement or loyalty metric determined by combining several of your key metrics. This will have to be determined by you as it depends on your industry and the specific type of service you provide.

Once you have established a growth pattern in loyalty you should be revisiting some of the site issues that are mentioned in "All Above the Fold" and "All About Speed." A successful campaign in visitor loyalty should create strong leaning in the type of users your site attracts. Look to the metric combinations that are used in the more design-heavy case studies to learn where you can reduce friction for your new loyal customers, and in the process you will make this type of customer more likely to convert from new visitor to return visitor.

Bringing These Ideas Together

The four examples we use are extremes of purpose. You will notice that "All Above the Fold" and "All About Speed" were largely focused on front end, appearance, and changes, while "All About the Customer" and "All About Retention" focused mainly on changes in service offering. What is right for your customers will definitely be a combination of things you offer and how you present information.

Our idea in mixing hypothetical and recognizable websites is that you as a reader can go look for yourself and consider not only the changes that we propose, but also notice what changes these sites actually make. The travel industry is an interesting early indicator for the web business as a whole. Because it was one of the first mainstream online industries to experience saturation, travel sites are dealing with many business issues that are not yet applicable to other businesses. Because they are well staffed and well funded, they can make some very large changes in both offering and design.

For example, when buyer confidence fades or fuel costs impact potential customers, you will see travel companies respond quickly. During certain times of the year you will see an increase in the use of guarantees, specials, and the like to overcome or capitalize on consumer buying tendencies.

Applying the concepts we have laid out to your website can help you make the same choices for your business. In choosing your brand's message and choosing your customers you should have an expanded tool set for solving problems and prioritizing what changes will create value for your business.

Now that you know what to look for when assessing your traffic and visitors it is time for you to apply it to your site. One of the biggest challenges in making customer-driven changes is trusting the information that you have. Asking people directly doesn't always provide real insight into their needs. Often they don't know what it is they are really looking for, even when they have an opinion. Asking yourself or your colleagues questions about what they want in a buying process can bring a good deal of insight to your decisions. Most of all, remember that you are trying to respond to behaviors. Imagine you are a user and think what questions you would be asking/looking to answer on a website.

Let's revisit some of the behaviors that you are trying to respond to in your website design and features.

- **A sense of accomplishment**
- **A feeling of being taken care of**
- **A connection to other people**
- **A sense of trust**
- **A thirst for information**

How Do People Who Are Hungry for Accomplishment Behave?

They exit quickly at roadblocks and they act quickly. If you have a series of short time on-page and then an exit, or a long time on-page, you are looking at a breakdown for Immediate and Competitive decision makers. You have halted their success.

What are the signs that you are not fulfilling this need?

- High Bounce Rate
- Long time on-site
- High page views
- Low conversion

How Do People Who Want to Be Taken Care of Behave?

They visit FAQs, contact, use forms, call/email, etc. If you are seeing lots of action in your administrative sections you have mostly relationship-driven users. If you also have low loyalty you are failing these people.

What are the signs that you aren't fulfilling this need?

- High exit from administrative sections
- Lots of time spent on-site followed by no conversion
- Low conversion and high call volume

How Do People Who Want a Connection to Other People Behave?

They spend time on testimonials and points of interactivity. If you see traction and attention in your contact and support details, or traction from pages that mention and exhibit satisfied customers, you have relationship-driven customers. How do you make them feel like they are really connecting with a person behind the site?

What are the signs that you aren't fulfilling this need?

- Low conversion and high call volume
- High number of complaints

- Low action on pages that lack pictures of people/comments by people

How Do People Who Want to Feel a Sense of Trust Behave?

They react strongly to professional endorsement: JD Power®, Consumer Reports©, Verisign®, etc. These people actually visit your guarantee and return policy. Everyone wants a little security; how do you provide it?

What are the signs that you aren't fulfilling this need?

- Low loyalty
- Low conversion
- High abandonment

How Do People Who Want Information Behave?

These users read your content and look at your pictures—they spend time and look around. They don't generally make contact, unless they are near a decision. Do you provide enough information that users can go from uninformed to informed in a single visit?

What are the signs that you aren't fulfilling this need?

- Low conversion
- High page views
- High time on-page/on-site

These are only some of the needs that your visitors are trying to fulfill on your site. Temperaments are only the context that people come from while trying to accomplish a goal. Think about some of the things you do in your daily life and match up what you need with how you behave, and how you satiate those needs.

Guidelines for Web Communications

Regardless of your intended conversion or the type of users you attract, the following are some general principles that will help your website communicate clearly with anyone.

1. Avoid Clutter

Users have a goal. If you have a lot going on—links, images, animation—the goal is harder to reach. White space is your friend. Leave some space, as in the Alpha Co. design, to let users know what is important; let your design support your call to action. Don't be afraid to use images and color, but make sure your design supports your primary user objective. Cart icons and telephone numbers are a good example of important information that becomes obscured when you have too much going on.

2. Create a Visual Path

Creating distinct levels of attention will help move users through your action path. But, if you have a number of elements that all ask for the same amount of attention none of them will be compelling. We know from endless eye tracking tests that people are going to start at the top of your page and move to subordinate elements. Advertising guru Joe Sugarman is well known for saying that every line you write is intended to pull you into the next line. Images can, and should, do the same.

3. Be Consistent About Everything...Almost

After only a few repetitions people build expectations. Help your users by fulfilling their expectations. Leave your navigation in the same place, lay down a trail to the next step, and make calls to action similar if they are on the same path

Don't go wild with fonts. Choose a serif and a sans serif to use in your headers, body, and graphics and use them the same way throughout your site. You don't need more than two fonts. Your body text should be 10 to 14 points tall to be readable. Be sparing with markup like bold and italics—the less you use them the more effect they have. Likewise be clear with your colors. Create a palette that contains only a couple of brand-distinctive colors and a neutral base across the site.

4. Break Color Scheme for Action Elements

Beautifully rendered, tasteful calls to action don't incite action. If you want action, make that element the most important thing on the page. Well-rendered is fine, but make it a color that stands out. Attract attention by making these elements incongruous in an otherwise harmonious layout.

5. Scanning, Not Reading

This entire section is built as a numbered list. You can get the same information from the bold heading as you do from reading the trailing text. Use captions on images, headers, and text markup to introduce the important points quickly and efficiently.

6. Put the Reading Somewhere

Some people do want every detail. In general, your visitors need more information than you think. Provide links to extended information where available; **do not use** "Click Here For More Information." That is meaningless without context. Use "More Information About_____." Now the user doesn't even need to read what precedes the link and the link passes some useful anchor text.

7. Build Content Top → Left → Right → Bottom

Follow the natural order of attention with your elements and you will achieve simple interaction that your users don't have to think about. Don't leave your important message at the bottom.

8. Streamline Your Processes (Don't Make Them Think)

There is an amazing book dedicated to this subject: *Don't Make Me Think* by Steven Krug. Every time your process stops, even for a second, your site experiences a loss of efficiency, and possibly a conversion. People have a great attention span when they know they are on the right path, but when the path becomes difficult or confusing, your visitors will become impatient.

9. Professional Work For Professional Results

The bottom line is that doing business on the Internet means taking the Internet seriously. If you treat your website as a business it will return the favor. For years companies have spent $10,0000-$100,000 to achieve noticeable, memorable placement in phone directories. Clearly those days are gone. Creating and maintaining a remarkable, usable website means investing in your resources: design, content, navigation, and advertising. You shouldn't blow the bank making a website, but remember that you get what you pay for.

Having guidelines will help you bring some common sense to your projects as you improve your site. Sometimes it is hard to remember what it is like being a user while you are making your changes. Match up goals with things that you can measure. Each of the nine ideas above addresses at least one basic need that is independent of product or service.

Take a moment at the beginning and end of the project to ask what problem you are looking to solve and what new problems you may be creating.

A Note for Small Businesses

As more industries become saturated, small businesses are going to be more hard pressed to act creatively. But, conceiving a great idea is not the only key to success in the future of the web. It is important that even small companies invest in clear communication of their value. If you are going to make the leap into doing business online, you should be putting your communication plans in place at the outset so your website can be a reliable channel while you work on other parts of your business.

The travel industry is a fairly saturated market, yet there continues to be a demand for new and alternative means of fulfilling travel needs. Some of the top trafficked travel aggregates are Expedia®, Hotwire™, Orbitz™, and Travelocity™. They all have the same pool of content and the same potential customer base. There are few barriers to toggling between one and another, so while the main goal of these websites is to generate a sale, the close secondary goal is to build a relationship and give users a reason to come back. It may seem like there are only four or five main options in your particular business pool and you have no way of tapping into this market; however, Kayak™ is an example of a small company that has been able to capitalize on a previously saturated market by offering a slightly different product. Their means of making money is different than most of its competition; however, their marketing plan seems to be tapping into the same pool of potential customers. They are an aggregator of aggregators selling leads instead of travel. At certain points throughout the year their web traffic rivals the aggregates listed above thanks to smart search engine marketing. By assessing the people who use travel aggregators and addressing one of their problems in a simple way, Kayak has tapped into what might be considered a previously saturated market, and generated revenue as well.

Kayak already incorporates several of our ideas into their website (though we are in no way affiliated with them). They are an All Above the Fold website and keep their landing page clean and simple. Also, they are an All About Speed website since the function unit is very easy to use and results are returned very quickly. In one aspect they are also an All About the Customer website—they tell you exactly what they are about in very simple text. They give you the option to choose one or more aggregators to gather information from. Finally, they utilize a session cookie so that if you do not find what you are looking for and go back to the landing page, they save your most recent search and search settings, making it easy for you to revise. So for an additional working example of how to incorporate some of our ideas please feel free to visit the Kayak website.

Build Some Traffic

In addition to the search channels discussed in the introduction, there are several great tools that aid in retaining customers. Your options include email subscription, RSS, widgets for Vista, iGoogle™, Pageflakes, Dashboard (OSX), a "make this page your home page" link, bookmarks, email a friend, wish list, and social media outlets.

Implementing email subscription is the most common way to gain a customer base. In fact, for many of you this may be your main function. However, for e-commerce sites email subscription provides a good indication of how many loyal customers you have, and allows you to send out email about new products, categories, site upgrades, and sales. We highly recommend that if you do use email advertising that you build or work with an email segmentation program.

Email subscription is a push marketing strategy that involves guessing what the customer might want to buy and advertising that to them, interrupting their life to give your message. A major downfall of this is that an email that doesn't make sense for the customer makes them less likely to pay attention in the future. As a customer there is nothing more annoying than constantly receiving email advertising that does not make sense for you. For instance, a woman is not very likely to open or click through an email for men's suits (unless she buys her husband's suits for him). Email segmentation should be more fully explored in other texts, but the better your email segmentation is the happier your customers will be and, more importantly, the more likely they are to open, click through, and make a purchase. You want to create a winning formula of visit, browse, buy, repeat. Creating a well-segmented email subscription option helps feed the formula by reducing the noise to signal in your push marketing.

If you are an email subscription site, you may be able to take advantage of some of what this chapter talks about, however you may want to focus on the other three types of changes that you can make on your site.

RSS technology employs a pull marketing technique that allows the visitor to subscribe to a headline format reader. He or she can view top stories for a website or customize and tailor to interest in a particular website. Typically the visitor will click on the RSS icon next to a category, story, or product and then indicate which RSS feeder they utilize and add the RSS to their feeder. This allows them to follow updates about your site or particular category or product on your site.

Widgets, in this instance, utilize RSS into an aggregator such as Vista, iGoogle™, Pageflakes, Dashboard (OSX). You may couple the link to a widget in the same section as your RSS. One of the best aspects of RSS for the customer is that it does not have the same feeling of spin, because it is a raw stream of data. Allowing users to tailor their information helps lower the barrier to re-entry and loyalty.

Bookmarks are the most widely used way of retaining visitors to your site, or possibly second to email subscription depending on your industry and service.

Bookmarks, which have been around since the first web browsers, allow users to save pages that they want to visit again.[1] Today, all web browsers

---

[1] http://en.wikipedia.org/wiki/Internet_bookmark

have some sort of favorites or bookmarking system, making repeat visits to a site very easy. Problems with bookmarking on early web browsers were a lack of visibility of the bookmarks section and lack of a coordinated bookmarking strategy. Early on, users were unable to find their bookmarked pages in the browser or, even worse, were unable to operate the bookmarking capability of the web browser.

Bookmarks have progressed over the years as web browsers have improved. The bookmarking function has been refined by the major browsers, allowing for things like folders and tags to create better organization. Now you can even connect your browser's bookmarks to web-based bookmark lists that you maintain on a website, making your bookmarks independent of your computer.

The only problem with bookmarks today is encouraging your visitor to utilize them. Many pages will incorporate a link stating "bookmark this page," however this is still a widely underused practice. Alternatives to bookmarks include, "email to a friend," "My Wishlist," RSS, or adding to a social networking tool.

The option to "email this page to a friend" has been around for some time but has never been an overly effective means of getting visitors to your site. This feature is mostly used for news stories.

The wish list option gives visitors to e-commerce sites an opportunity to compile a list of things that they would like to have, but cannot or do not want to buy for themselves.

Social media tools such as StumbleUpon, Digg™, Delicious, and Reddit allow visitors and customers to post a link for their peer group to view, visit, and/or comment on. Using these venues runs you the risk of allowing the public to comment on your site and/or having a large number of unconvertible visitors sent to your site. If these viewers enjoy your site this can be a huge additional traffic and conversion boost for you. However, if they do not like your site, you will see an immediate conversion drop and repeat visits and repeat visitor conversion could also drop if a large negative campaign is written about your site. It is important to bear in mind that social media is not an appropriate venue for hard selling. If you are not prepared to participate socially, you will be better served by spending time in a different channel.

Analytics are good for more than tracking. They can be used to help define your strategy to incorporate strengths that you were not aware of. Looking into your analytics before you start keyword research can be very valuable in choosing your target terms intelligently.

Here are some commonly available metrics you can use to expand organic search campaigns:

1. **Referring Domains**—who sends your traffic? Major search engines often make up a large percentage of traffic for many sites. However, you should also pay attention to other sites send referrals. Your referrals can help by introducing you to site themes and business verticals that you may be able to generate buzz through. Knowing your audience is critical in making design, function, and business offerings.

2. **Referring Keywords**—millions of people are using search engines each day. That means there are searches that will never cross your mind to target that you just naturally accumulate because of your content or writing. Search your logs to find these frequent constructions

that may help you expand your visibility and better focus where you point your campaigns in the future. Specifically separate out looking phrases, researching phrases, and buying phrases.

3. **Click Paths**—if you see many people end up in the same section or page of your site within a few clicks, it indicates that you have an opportunity to engage people more effectively by creating more targeted content for that theme. This was covered several times in the section about site reviews, but it is also useful for expansion of search traffic.

4. **Paid vs. Natural Search**—any phrases that are popular in one channel should be considered for addition to the other channel.

5. **Geographic Referrals**—for marketing campaigns that include offline advertising, geo targeting is very important to establish results. You can pair the airing (printing) of offline promotions with changes in traffic by region. When you section out these groups you may find opportunities to create region-specific promotions (landing pages or service offerings) to maximize your value. For industries like travel that already have a strong geographic component, regional segmentation can be an informative process for determining changes.

6. **Visiting Trends**—tracking seasonality is a frequently overlooked metric. Your visitor trends should be analyzed in relation to expected changes in your business. You should compare current trends with past trends, search trends, and economic trends to get the most value. Keeping your expected trends in mind will give you a leg up when setting benchmarks for assessing your post-change data.

7. **Top Landing Pages**—we use the home page for our site reviews, but your analytics will give you more ideas for pages to apply changes to. The first step in determining your top landing pages should be to compartmentalize your data. Look at organic, paid, and referral traffic separately. Landing page should also be paired with click path; if you are creating common paths you should be looking at how to improve customer experience along that path. Additionally you want to work on better targeting the page content to the desired conversion. This will improve both your paid and organic results for your desired actions.

8. **Bounce Rate**—this metric tracks how many people arrive on a page and immediately leave. Good bounce rates vary greatly depending on your vertical and traffic source. What is important in determining this value is to pair bounce rate with another metric. Find a connection so you can make a clear assessment of what aspect of the page is losing the customer. It may be that users can't find what they want, that some portion of your page is broken, or a number of other issues. The important information you get from bounce rate is largely in conjunction with another metric.

Make Your Analysis in Context

It is rare that you will have a stable set of data to measure against. Seasonality, site growth, and external events will all have a major effect on your returns. Seasonally, Internet usage fluctuates; it is usually lower in the summer, for example, and business-specific events will throw new variables into your data.

Don't discard tests unless you know why they failed. You need to make sure your test data is compared not only to the recent past, but also to seasonal data from your past and any incidental events in your industry.

There will also be times that you choose the correct elements to change, but still won't see a positive result. Pairing performance indicators will help you assess whether you have made a partially correct decision that has the potential to become positive. An example from earlier: you change text in a call to action and it increases entrance into your conversion funnel but doesn't increase total conversion. Is this good or bad? Strictly based on conversion you haven't gained ground, but reversing the element would be a mistake. In this case you should examine the element and the destination. Either the call to action needs to be changed to better match the process or the destination needs to incorporate the new call. When examining your post-change data, make some comparisons between coupled performance indicators to expand the information you get, even from negative changes.

Do Some User Testing

User testing doesn't have to be complicated or extended to be useful, it just has to be focused. You only need a handful of people to get a sense of what your changes affect. If you have a handful of friends or co-workers who aren't involved in the project, you can use JavaScript to set a cookie specifically for them to track their use of the new version. What you most want to focus on is giving them a specific task on the site and comparing their data on your performance indicators with what you would like to see.

This simple act can give you some clear context for what your data means, especially if you pair it with the following questions:

What was the easiest part of your task?

What was the hardest part of your task?

Where you successful in completing your task?

What would make your task simpler?

If you can get six people to perform the task and answer the questions, you probably can acquire an important piece of information. Now ask the following questions when you look at your user tests:

How do users behave in the *most confusing parts of your site?*

- Do they slow down?
- Visit multiple times?
- Visit shortly and never return?

Does anyone claim to have been successful in spite of not meeting your criteria for success?

Does anyone feel unsuccessful in spite of meeting your performance criteria?

Your testing definitely can be more comprehensive than this, but these simple questions can give you a quick and dirty look at what you have done to your users in a more accessible way than raw data.

Setting up a simple test using Google™ Analytics to track the test group separately from everyone else would look like this.

On a designated start page for the test, use the following body tag:

```
<body onLoad="JavaScript:pageTracker._setVar('user_test);">
```

You can now filter out all data that is not from your test subjects. Consult your analytics provider or manual to learn more about how you can set a cookie and filter for these kinds of tests.

Think About Methods, Not Band-Aids

Don't be scared by tests that don't yield immediate positive results. If you have defined a good set of performance indicators you can still end with valuable data that helps you make the best decisions as you make changes in the future. When you renovate your site you are looking to grow into your customers. Building traffic will result in a stream of people and analytics will help you learn who they are. Your job is to respond to their needs and solidify the relationship by capitalizing on the information they give you.

As use of the Internet expands, even niche and local businesses are going to find increasing saturation in their verticals. Now is the time to differentiate yourself from your competitors. Take your brand seriously on the Web and recognize that the same aspects of the Web that give you expanded potential also give you an expanded, and perhaps invisible, supply of competition. Your job as an analyst, marketer, or web designer is to expand the value of your website to serve at least one type of client very well. If you wait until differentiation is a live or die issue you will have a harder time overcoming the obstacles to being remarkable in your space.

Start now by finding the quiet messages that your visitors are sending about themselves and taking small steps toward being loved by some group of users. Take for example Myspace® and Facebook®.

Myspace® quite literally made YouTube™ valuable. The inclusion of YouTube videos on Myspace increased the value to Myspace users—in turn the volume of users turned YouTube into something worth using and buying. But who does Myspace serve? Is it about music? Connecting to people you used to know? Or is it an advertising vehicle for NewsCorp?

In contrast, Facebook®, was created to serve a specific community—students—and has expanded based on its service of their needs. The early days of exclusivity and focus have allowed them to develop a clear brand that gives them value above and beyond their competitor. Even though their growth has precipitated, they are able to distance themselves from some of the same issues that plague MySpace in part by continuing to cater to their core audience.

It is our hope that looking through our examples has provided you with new ideas for approaching the development of your business and website. We invite you to join us at UserDrivenChange.com to share in further discussion on the topic to help you better understand not just who is using your site, but how you can better serve their needs and make them part of your online community.

Glossary of Terms

Customer Opinion Data—this can be a feedback link hosted by your site or by a third party—an index tool such as Nielsen Netratings. This is typically termed qualitative data.

Direct Navigation (no referrer)—referrer type in marketing; in this case the referrer value is empty or null; it is assumed to indicate that the visitor directly entered the URL or selected it from a list of bookmarks, but this is not always the case. If the user agent does not set the proper referrer value in the request header, it will be collected as null or unknown.

Engagement Metrics—used to describe the behavior of a visitor on your website. Possible metrics include recency, frequency, page exit ratio, bounce rate, pages per visit, elements per visit, and conversions per visit.

Exit Page—the last page on a site accessed during a visit, signifying the end of a visit/session.

Key Performance Indicators (KPIs)—these are typically determined by your company and/or industry vertical. Possible metrics include visits (sessions), conversion, sales, average order size.

Page Exit Ratio—the number of exits from a page divided by the total number of page views of that page.

Pathing Analysis/Click Stream Reporting—typically this is a report found in your analytics tool that allows you to see the most common path to or from a specific page on your site. In some analytics tools you have the option to determine a set path to find out the completion percentage on each step of the path. (These may be two separate reports.)

Popover--may also be called a modal window. An alternative to a popup, it is designed to counter popup blockers. Popovers are not really a window but rather just another layer on the page itself

Single Page Visits (Bounces)—a visit that consists of one page view.

Site Exit Surveys—typically hosted by a third party, these can be popups that occur once you leave a site (but do not close your browser). Generally these are in a multiple question format or a ratings format. The data is compiled to find out about the visitor's shopping experience.

Time Spent On-page—the length of time on a page. Calculation is typically the timestamp of when the visitor leaves the page minus the timestamp of when the visitor left the previous page. Entry pages typically are not able to be calculated since there is no tag thrown prior to entering the site. (While not an official metric of the WAA publication, this metric can be found in many analytics platforms.)

Visit Duration—the length of time in a session. Calculation is typically the timestamp of the last activity in the session minus the timestamp of the first activity of the session.

Index

Analysis, 13, 40, 59, 83, 100
Analysis in Context, 123

Bookmarks, 119–20
Bounce Rate, 41, 42, 60, 61, 84, 123, 129

Click Path Analysis, 63
Click Path Reporting, 105
Click Paths, 122
Click Paths Report, 49
Conversion Path Completion, 105
Conversion Starts, 48
Customer Types, 20–24

Direct Navigation, 128

Exit Page, 128
Exit Surveys, 106

Feedback Forums, 106
Function Unit Submits, 47, 62, 88, 106

Geographic Referrals, 122

KPI's (Key Performance Indicators), 9

Landing Page, 85, 105
Landing Page Tactics, 14–17
Landing Page Types, 17–19

Offline Advertising, 32
Organic Search, 26–30

Page Views, 46, 64, 85
Pages Per Visit, 46, 64, 85, 103
Paid Search, 30–31
Paid vs. Natural Search, 122
Pathing Analysis, 128
Popover, 129

Referring Domains, 121
Referring Keywords, 121

Segmentation Analysis, 101
Site Conversion, 50, 65, 89
Site Exits, 43, 65, 129

Top Landing Pages, 123

Usability Testing, 99
User Testing, 124

Visiting Trends, 122
Visitor to Buyer Path Completion, 86
Visual Communication, 113

About The Authors

Jeff Noethen is a Web Analyst for a high end fashion retailer with three years of Web Analytics and Usability experience. He also has four years of sales and customer service experience for both online and in store companies. He has over 18 years of self taught computer experience and over 12 years of Internet experience. He co-operated a part time independent computer help desk business while in college. Jeff has worked for several small businesses, as well as several large corporations including American Express. While he currently resides in Seattle, WA, he grew up in Texas and has a degree in International Business, a minor in Business Administration and Spanish, and a Latin American Business Certificate from Texas State University. While this is his first major published work, Jeff has written opinion pieces and sports recaps for his university newspaper, and has several personal blogs.

Carlos del Rio is the founder and chief consultant of Agillian, a search marketing company, based in Seattle that provides search marketing, web analytics, and usability services. He has over 12 years self-taught computer and Internet experience. He has served as Pay Per Click and Affiliate manager for eMerchandise and VizMedia, LLC, PPC Manager and SEO Specialist for Visible Technologies, LLC and Point It Search Marketing, and as an Educational Instructor for YMCA of America and AmeriCorps. Carlos currently lives in Seattle, WA, and grew up in Las Vegas. He holds a Bachelor of Arts from Reed College in Portland Oregon. This is Carlos' first major publishing, but his other writing can be seen around the web on subjects ranging from search marketing to humor.

www.ingramcontent.com/pod-product-compliance
Ingram Content Group UK Ltd.
Pitfield, Milton Keynes, MK11 3LW, UK
UKHW050411240426
12048UKWH00020B/1454